Also by
Rabbi Adin Steinsaltz

The Talmud: The Steinsaltz Edition
(available in Hebrew, English, French, and Russian)
The Thirteen-Petalled Rose
The Essential Talmud
Strife of the Spirit
Biblical Images
Talmudic Images
The Long Shorter Way: Discourses on Chasidic Thought
In the Beginning: Discourses on Chasidic Thought
The Sustaining Utterance: Discourses on Chasidic Thought
The Candle of God: Discourses on Chasidic Thought
On Being Free
The Tales of Rabbi Nachman of Bratslav
Teshuvah: A Guide for the Newly Observant Jew
The Woman of Valor
The Passover Haggadah

Thinking
About
What Really
Matters in Life

Simple Words

❧

Adin Steinsaltz

Edited by Elana Schachter and Ditsa Shabtai

Simon & Schuster Paperbacks
New York London Toronto Sydney

SIMON & SCHUSTER PAPERBACKS
A Division of Simon & Schuster, Inc.
1230 Avenue of the Americas
New York, NY 10020

Copyright © 1999 by Adin Steinsaltz

This Simon & Schuster trade paperback edition July 2008

SIMON & SCHUSTER PAPERBACKS and colophon are
registered trademarks of Simon & Schuster, Inc.

For information about special discounts for bulk purchases,
please contact Simon & Schuster Special Sales at
1-800-456-6798 or business@simonandschuster.com

Designed by Karolina Harris

Manufactured in the United States of America

1   3   5   7   9   10   8   6   4   2

The Library of Congress has cataloged
the hardcover as follows:

Adin Steinsaltz.

p.   cm.

Includes bibliographical references.

1. Conduct of life.   2. Spiritual life.
3. Spiritual life—Judaism.   I. Title.

BJ1581.2.S742   1999

296.3—dc21   99-16995   CIP

ISBN-13: 978-0-684-84642-2
ISBN-10:   0-684-84642-X
ISBN-13: 978-1-4165-5697-8 (pbk)
ISBN-10:   1-4165-5697-4 (pbk)

Through the kindness of the Nathan Cummings Foundation, this book is dedicated to the memory of my grandparents Simy and Abraham Dahan, who shared their wisdom and generosity with all who knew them.

May Simple Words *resonate into the heart and soul of every man and woman and strengthen our shared humanity.*

—SONIA SIMON-CUMMINGS

Contents

Simple
Words

Preface

Words, words, words, so many of them, spoken and written, printed and screened, seen on the Internet and as graffiti on walls. There are also words that are whispered, and those that we never say.

This book is about words, but not about clever, sophisticated words such as "internalization," or long, technical ones like "dimethylcarbinol"; it is about some of the meanings of simple, everyday words.

Simple words are by no means simple. In fact, many of the simple words and notions that we use contain very complex ideas. Understanding the meaning of a word is not achieved by finding its Sanskrit or Latin root, but by grasping clearly what it is that we say or think in a blurred way. Science, even in its most advanced form, is founded upon pondering the meaning of the simplest terms: line, number, weight, air.

This book looks into some basic, common words somewhat like peeking through a hole in a hedge. New dimensions appear in commonly used words, boundaries become better defined, and the contents become more important.

This is not a preaching book. To the extent that it has a message, it is a very humble one: understand better what you are saying; there is more in you than you imagine. The hidden wisdom of commonplace words is sometimes startling, not because it is novel, but because it is somehow known to us.

This book was conceived years ago, in 1982, during my stay at the Institute for Advanced Study in Princeton, when I had the double luxury of working very hard and loafing. Since then, the main ideas went through a process of deliberation and change. With the help of the Aleph Society in New York, and the diligence of Robbie Martz there, the chapters of this book were delivered as talks to various audiences in the United States; some face-to-face, most as teleconferences from Jerusalem.

I wish to thank the participants for their patience, as well as for their comments and criticisms, and even for their facial expressions. Many of their observations were later incorporated into the book.

Thanks to the very hard work of my editors, Elana Schachter and Ditsa Shabtai, and the helpful comments of Margy-Ruth Davis, the transcripts of these talks were transformed into the chapters of this book.

Words

ə

M a n k i n d can best be defined as "the speaking species."
Nature traditionally has been divided into four classes: the
inanimate world; the flora, or plant world; the fauna, or animal world; and mankind, called "the speaker." Man the
speaker is a separate class. The scientific definition of man
as *Homo sapiens* is not the best title for humanity; many animals—dolphins, for example—also have high levels of in-
telligence, perhaps not too inferior to that of humans. In
addition, man's attempts at wisdom have not always been
successful. However, the fact that we are speakers is basic,
so very primal that it differentiates us from the rest of creation. The right name for us should be, perhaps, *Homo gar-
rulus*. This title is not facetious; it defines not only man's
distinction, but also his superiority.

It is not just that we can communicate; everything can

communicate. The birds and the bees, and even plants, can transmit some signals to each other, by voice, by sight, or by scent, but ours is a very different form of communication. As far as we know, animals can only transmit emotions, or status reports. They can signal statements such as, "Here I am," "I am about to attack you," or "I am going to court you"—depending on the situation. Humans can create words, which are transmittable symbols. We can create symbols for everything in the world: objects, space, and time, concrete notions and abstract ones, ideas and emotions. We can talk about almost everything in the world, and give it a name.

The Book of Genesis tells us about the creation of Man. The Midrash, in Genesis *Rabbah,* a fourth-century homiletic exegesis on the Bible, says that God consulted the angels about the creation of Man, and the angels did not like the idea at all.[1] To them, connecting a Divine soul with an earthly body seemed a strange and unlikely combination, bound to fail. The Midrash[2] then goes on to tell that after Man was created, God showed the new world and all its creatures to the angels, and asked, "Can you give names to all these things around you?" The angels said they could not. Then God showed off His new creature, Man, to prove his special qualities; all the animals passed before Adam, and Adam gave names to each one (Genesis 2:19)—including himself,[3] his wife (Genesis 2:23), and the Almighty.[4] That was the beginning of Man as a distinctive creation, different indeed from all other creatures, superior to animals and even to angels—not merely because he can talk, but because of the ability to create words.

This "gift of gab" is useful: we use words to transmit pictures, frames of mind, information, emotions. However, we are not just users of words—we are their creators. Some of us begin creating words at the age of two and finish at the age of three; some of us go on creating words—by chance or by will—throughout our lives. Words come from that deep place where each of us is a creator. Man the speaker is the only creature who can use words to represent objects or ideas. Of course, man can do many other things—with his hands and with other parts of himself. However, the critical difference, the big jump, is man's ability to transfer, to communicate an idea from one person to another by the symbols, words, that he creates. This ability to transmit knowledge, to transfer information and experience to others, and to advance through the generations is the basis of all culture.

The words that we use outwardly are only a part of those we use inwardly. We not only talk to each other with words, we also think with words. It may be possible that at a certain level we think without words. The basic, primordial thought process is not made up of distinct words, but is rather a mental collage composed of different symbols. We feel emotions, we have ideas that we get in a flash, which come to some of us as complete pictures, and to others as sounds, echoes, or smells. Then we go through a process of completion, of formation, which puts the idea into words. Most of us, however, do even our internal, deep-level thinking using words.

Words are vehicles, and very powerful ones. To use an ancient metaphor, the connection between the idea and the word can be compared to the relationship between a person and a horse. The horse is far more powerful and much faster than the person, but it must be harnessed and guided. The combination man-horse is a very different thing from each of them as an individual being. For the Aztecs, for instance, the first sight of a man on a horse was a shock. This united being with four legs, two hands, two heads, and so on was formidable, frightening, almost God-like.

We ride our words, but words have a tremendous power of their own. They form a vehicle that makes the person within it a different being. There is a complex connection between the thinking, dreaming, daydreaming self, and the words used to express that self, from the simplest "I am hungry," "I want," "I love," or "I hate," to the most complicated ideas. For beyond being our creations, words are also our creators. The way we are, our thinking processes, the ways we react, are created by our collection of words. "The soul is full with words";[5] so much so that some people believe that each person gets an allocation of words for a lifetime, and once it is used up, life ends.

The meaning of a word has a power of its own. Words give us the enormous power of transferring ideas to others, even as words help us formulate ideas in ways that we ourselves can grasp. When we understand words—not as history or as a dictionary definition, but as living entities—when we grasp both the power and the limits of words, that is the basis of a new relationship with our own ideas.

Sometimes we are at a loss for words, and not just because of the common phenomenon of forgetting a word; we just cannot find a way to express certain feelings. Much more often, however, we use words frivolously, or are hampered and confined by our words. Words can have multiple uses and meanings. Individual and cultural differences sometimes reveal themselves in differences in the words that we use. Regional differences, as well as social class stratification, are created and manifested by using different words, and by giving them different meanings. In some primitive tribes, there are different dialects for man-language and woman-language, which are almost incomprehensible to each other, but even when men and women use exactly the same language, gender differences sometimes give the same words very different meanings.[6] When the meaning gap is big enough, then we may speak about the same things, we may even have the same dictionary definitions, and still the words may not be refined enough to clarify the differences between one person's use of language and another's.*

Sometimes, cultural or personal misunderstandings occur when people use the same word but with slightly different meanings. Misunderstanding can also be a matter of context. Hearing a child say, "I hate you," is not

*Sometimes, it is a matter of the general and the particular. Just as some languages have names for many shades of a color, while in other languages there are only a few, some languages have words for shades of meaning that other languages can only express in a generalized or clumsy way.

quite the same as hearing the same words from the other end of a gun. Sometimes, the misuse of words is done intentionally. Talleyrand used to say, "Speech was given to Man in order to lie." Lying can be done effectively just by an intentional misuse of words, but many times people lie unconsciously, or semiconsciously.

There are weak words, strong words, ambiguous words. There are also words frequently overused and abused—the most prominent example being, perhaps, the word "love." "Love" means many different, sometimes contradictory things, which are all put in one shell; yet it is this shell that we deal with, that we think with, and sometimes we get confused by. Some words are very intimate, because we use them not only with others, but also with ourselves. By trying to find all the connotations we are not only learning more about the meaning of a word: we are also grappling with our ideas.

One of the problems facing us today is the invasion of daily speech by professional, semiscientific jargon. It is not the number of jargon words in the dictionary that matters, but the way people use them in communicating with each other, and therefore—on a different level—also in the way they deal with themselves. Jargon, in the sense of professional language, is a kind of shorthand; it takes various notions, some of which may be rather complex, and puts them in one word or in a short phrase. As such, jargon may be very helpful, but it is best used where it is meant to be used, namely, within the realm of the profession, where those who use these terms ostensibly know what they are saying. When used more widely, in a different and possibly inaccurate or misleading context, they are often misunderstood.

People often speak about "order of magnitude," when they should simply say "big" or "small"; or they speak about "relativity," when they want to say "not exactly." In America, and possibly also in Europe, there is an increasing use of psychological jargon, which is replacing other words. People no longer love each other: they have a relationship. They do not hate: they have a negative set of reactions. They do not have problems: they have complexes. These complexes even have names, some of them quite fancy, but actually, they are all feelings and emotions, and their real existence may be likewise painful.*

Mark Twain lists eighteen rules that a certain writer violated, one of them being, "Use the right word, not its second cousin." When it comes to jargon, this kind of violation is very common. We use first and second cousins because we do not know the real meaning of the word. People who get caught by the jargon find themselves saying things that are quite different from what they really mean, or even worse, they cease to know what they mean altogether.

The problem with jargon goes beyond that. In his famous book *1984*, George Orwell writes about the subject of forming people's thinking by creating a special language. A language in which certain words do not exist, and other

---

I myself coined at least one name for a very common complex: the Jewish Mother Syndrome. I call it the Jocasta Complex, the counterpart of the Oedipus Complex.

words have only a stipulated, jargon meaning, creates people who can talk, but are unable to think—at least not about certain things. When there is no word for something, either one has to invent a word, or—more commonly—one is stuck, because of the inability to think about an idea. People are even more stuck when they are given substitute words, especially ones that catch on easily. For then, instead of saying what they really want to say, people settle for something that is close enough, but not quite the same.

Once people begin to internalize this shorthand, to use it on themselves, they gradually lose their simple, basic ways of relating; they take complex jargon formulas as substitutes for simple words. It is not just a matter of replacing certain words with more beautiful ones. Many words have synonyms with almost the same meaning, the only difference being a subtle linguistic distinction. Jargon, however, not only changes the words, it changes their inner meaning; it biases our thinking. People end up using artificial constructs instead of natural ones, complex words instead of simple words, and become unable to say what they really want to say.

Take some examples from other spheres of life: we could, if we wished, avoid the trouble of eating by being fed intravenously. It is quite easy, very mechanical, not even painful, and it is effective, in the sense that one gets all the liquid and nourishment one needs; but one also loses the joy and taste of eating. Another example would be mechanical procreation. It could be much faster and more efficient, would save lots of effort and prevent the birth of unwanted children, but this would not be just a change of means; it is an essential change. A purely mechanical, pre-structured world such as this is a totally different world. Luckily, we have not yet been completely taken over by me-chanical jargon forms, yet we do use them, and, in a sense, are used by them.

Jargon language might, perhaps, be smoother, but it can turn our words into something like mechanically grown vegetables: bigger, with all the right colors, but with a taste that is not the same. To use a different metaphor: the difference between simple words and jar-gon terms is the difference between the sound of a violin, with its many overtones and undertones, and an artifi-cially created pure tone.

Just as there is a deep problem of becoming confused, mistaken, mechanical, and untrue by using jargon, there are also problems in using simple words. The richness and awesome complexity that exist in many natural, sim-ple, well-known things are also found in basic, simple words—which are also those words that we usually learn earliest. These are, in fact, not simple at all. They have the same seeming simplicity as the smallest flower grow-ing in the field, which is far more complex than the most advanced mechanism. Like the smell of fresh-baked bread, which has many nuances, and is far more complex than an artificial scent made in a factory according to a formula, simple words have many components and conno-tations, and they have an enormous emotional impact. Like other natural things, they grow. We learn them when we are babies, and we keep modifying them throughout our lives.

Words for basic notions, feelings, and reactions are the words that are most important to us: Love, Hate, Friendship, Family, God, Man, Justice. We think with them at a primitive, very powerful level. A girl counting flower petals, "He loves me, he loves me not," is actually asking, "What is love? What kind of love? What does each of us mean when we speak of love?" When we say, "I love you," "I hate you," "I want to marry you," "I want to be your friend," "I curse God," "I bless God," "I praise," "I blaspheme"—we are using words that, in many cases, we do not really understand. Because we know these words for such a long time, because we seem to know their meaning so well, we never have the chance to really understand what they mean. When we grapple with the meaning of the words, we discover what they are. Through this process of trying to understand, the words may become very different; sometimes we also gain a new understanding of ourselves and what we have been doing all our lives. This understanding is itself a revelation.

In Molière's play *The Bourgeois Gentleman,* the hero says, "Fancy that! I have been speaking prose all my life, and I never knew it." It is very true. With many of the words we use daily, we talk poetry, or philosophy, or theology, and we know it not; we say lots of nonsense without knowing it, and also lots of wisdom—with the same kind of ignorance.

We do not have to go to the other side of the world and hear strange new words in order to realize that there are things within ourselves that we do not know anything about. The real quest is to understand the words that we use constantly, for these are the foundation of our existence. What are they? What are they made of? These words, as powerful as they are, are also very foggy. They have a meaning for each of us, but what precisely is that meaning? Clarifying our understanding of simple words will not just change our way of speaking; it will also change our way of thinking and change our basic feelings. When we know certain things about those words, we become different people; we are re-created.

The exploration of simple words undertaken in this book is, in a certain way, a discussion about the creation of Man—which brings us back to the beginning of this chapter. The Midrashic account says that Man and Woman were first created as one body; later God cut that being in half, thereby making a separate Man and a separate Woman.[7]

What was Adam and Eve's greatest discovery when they were cut apart? It was, possibly, like looking in a mirror: "Bone of my bones and flesh of my flesh" (Genesis 2:23)—yet something different. It was also the first time that Adam and Eve could begin to have a conversation. When I speak with another being who is similar to me, yet different, I begin not only to understand the other, but also to understand what I myself am speaking about.

I do not know what language Adam spoke with Eve, with the animals, or with the angels; but I am sure it was simple words.

Nature

❧

T h e word "nature" is one of the fuzzy words that are used—and abused—to express many diverse concepts and meanings. It may be used to describe the existing order, but there are other common usages in which Nature is spelled with a capital N. Due to atheistic (or agnostic) coyness, it sometimes means almost the same thing as God. The ever popular "Mother Nature" is only one of the ways in which the term is personalized and idealized.

Two of the more formal definitions are closely linked. Nature is the totality of existence. Anything and everything, from the mightiest galaxies to the smallest subatomic particles, the whales and the lice, all are parts of nature. Nature also comprises all the laws of existence, the rules by which all the parts operate, and the relationships among them. In a slightly broader sense, nature is the usual order of things, which keeps on going as long as nothing interferes with it.

Naturalists, the people engaged in studying natural sciences, are probably the people who use the word "nature" most rarely. They are busy with their studies and are frequently too immersed in detail to have the time and inclination to use this all-encompassing (and rather vague) term. However, nature and natural laws are far more important to other human beings. The questions we pose are not about nature per se, but rather about our relationship with nature. Humanity can be in harmony with nature, in conflict with nature, or indifferent to nature—these are some of our choices. Such choice is not an abstract problem; we face it whenever we build a city or weed a garden, when we light a cigarette or educate a child.

The first thing that has to be remembered is that we humans are part of the natural world. Often, either for valid reasons or because we are arrogant and egocentric, we view ourselves as separate and distinct from the rest of creation. We speak about "humanity" and "nature" as if we exist in one way, and the rest of the world exists in a different way. This dichotomy between man and nature is neither simple nor accurate. Granted, nature without the presence of man would be very different; yet humanity, although unique and distinct, is still part of nature. Whether we define nature as the totality of existence, or as the set of laws that govern it—we are included in it.

The obvious notion that humanity is a part of nature

has some startling ramifications. We say that nature is silent; nature follows its course; nature does not care about people; nature does not have intentions; nature does not have purpose; nature does not have thought. However, we are part of nature, and we have all these traits. Nature, as it manifests in a storm, does not think and does not feel, but nature as it manifests in animals feels pain, attraction, hunger. Nature as it manifests in humanity thinks, writes poetry, and prays. Could we say that man is not a thinking creature because his hands and feet do not think? One part of the whole is a thinking part, and therefore we say that man is a thinking creature, a feeling creature. In the same way, we have to say that nature feels, thinks, is purposeful, and does right and wrong, insofar as we humans do those things.

On the other hand, it is also clear that there is a difference between humans and the rest of nature. Even without discussing the theological question of whether we have souls while other creatures do not (or, if animals do have souls, whether human souls are superior), and while setting aside the question of whether other creatures can think about their actions, still, humans are distinct from other creatures.

The primary distinction is that, from our very creation, we have free will, which we exercise through the many choices we make. While the rest of nature seems to be bound by rigid laws (of physics and chemistry), or by instincts and reflexes, we are not bound by our innate nature in the same way as other creatures in the world. A sheep cannot decide to begin hunting and eating other animals, and even a well-behaved tiger cannot decide to become vegetarian because of humane (or tigerish) considerations. We, as people, can choose whether to prey on others or to graze.

Furthermore, according to an anthropological definition, man is a creator of tools. Since we have tools, which enormously enhance our power, we change nature considerably, and at will; consequently, we have the freedom to move around, to live underground or above ground, to build and to destroy, to create bizarre things that never existed before. Man is also the creator of words; since we have words and language, we can conceive elaborate plans, transmit them to other people and other generations, and thereby change nature.

Our distinction from other parts of nature is apparent in our behavior as well. We do many things that no other animal does; for instance, we dress. Also, we are the only creatures that kill our own species en masse; that is also unnatural. Ever since the beginning of our existence, we have exercised our ability—whose boundaries are expanding daily—to change things at will. Our free will is sometimes frivolous, often foolish, but in any case, it pushes us to try, and sometimes to do, many new things. We have managed to form and destroy a great number of things, and we are still creating and innovating.

We have even succeeded in turning our basic weakness into strength. Biologically, we are not specialized; other creatures far surpass us in almost every capacity. They are better at running, jumping, swimming, climbing, and so many other skills. All our senses are inferior to those of other creatures. Even our brain lacks many special capacities. We cannot find our homes like dogs; we cannot navigate like birds; we cannot move in the dark like bats. Yet we have created, with our rather clumsy fingers, tools and machines that enable us to outrun the cheetah, to outfly the eagle, to outspin the spider.

The natural world can be seen as a vast orchestra in which each of the creatures has a distinct voice and sound. A drum and a flute are not interchangeable. The spider can produce threads; the bee cannot. We humans made ourselves, somehow, into a combination of all the creatures, and we can do everything. We can make honey and we can sting; we can plant and we can destroy; we can kill and we can resuscitate. All these abilities are part of our strange, diverse nature.

Our power of choice enables us to do things for our good and our benefit, and also things that are against our best interests. A baby goat will not jump down from a high rock unless it can do so without being hurt. It has an instinct for self-preservation. A baby human cannot be trusted in the same way:[1] a child might jump or creep down and be injured. We can rely on an apple tree not to produce oranges, but we cannot rely on a human to be consistent. According to the ancient explanation, this is because humans have both good and evil inclinations. Nowadays we would say it is because we humans have cut ourselves loose from the total rule of instinct, and instead, we have the ability to make both good and bad choices.

Of course, we may say that the question "What is natural?" is of no importance. Why should we bother about it? We change things, but so does every other creature, from a microbe or a virus, to a plant, to a complex animal. The bee makes pollen into honey; the simplest plants take air, water, soil, and sunshine and make them into fruit; locusts can devastate a country, and beavers can flood valleys. Why is all that considered natural, while some of our actions are not?

The difference is quantitative. In the course of many generations, our abilities have grown to surpass those of almost any creature. The quantity of changes can become qualitative, and cause irreversible results. Creating a vast new lake, or destroying species, are not intrinsically different from what other creatures do, but the dimensions of the event have many more implications. What is more important, however, is that our flexibility and our free choice—even in the narrow limits within which our physical existence can be sustained—make it possible for us to do amazing things, some of which no other creature can do. We can create permanent radioactivity, we can genetically engineer. Our emotional and spiritual capacity is even broader than our physical existence, and therefore we can do even more in those realms. We do not know the full extent of what we can do, nor all of the sometimes frightening, sometimes uplifting, always surprising consequences of our actions.

Our freedom compels us to be more, rather than less, careful about what we do, because we have the power to do so much. The need for deliberation about our deeds goes further than general caution. If we make changes which are too abrupt, or go against the grain, or exceed a certain limit, we damage the fabric of existence. For even if we believe that nature does not care about good and evil, it seems that nature does care about sustaining basic forms of life. Certain things that we have created go against nature—not because they are impossible, but because they go against this sustaining flow. We have to keep within certain boundaries; if we do not, we may kill ourselves, both physically and psychologically.

Our bad luck is that our excesses may not kill us immediately. We know, from our experience as a species as well as from personal experience, that nature does not always react immediately. Leaning over an abyss may not immediately result in a fall; a child playing with matches may have some time to enjoy the fire before he gets burned. In a similar way, we do not have the same reaction that animals have to poison, or, for that matter, to wrong; we can digest both. Therefore, we can harm ourselves physically and morally without knowing that we are doing so—until the inevitable results.

This is the reason we need to figure out what the natural laws and regulations are and by which ones we humans must abide. In the realm of our physical deeds, we now have a whole body of knowledge—although still far from perfect, and sometimes quite inconclusive—about ecology. This subject is developing, and becoming increasingly popular, because of the fear that we may step out of the boundaries, and eventually destroy ourselves. The same problem exists also in regard to our behavior and way of life. Some of the many things that we can do mentally are still within the boundaries of nature, or at least of our part of it; others may go against the general flow, and eventually destroy us.

The fundamental question, then, is, should we move "back to nature," should we stay where we are, or should we develop even more? Should we correct nature, change nature, destroy nature? Should we do all those artificial things that are humanly possible?

This question, which was never a theoretical one, has become even more critical in our time, when artifacts—those things that we build which are not "natural"—are becoming increasingly powerful. We have to decide how "natural" we should be. It begins with as simple a question as whether a woman should wear makeup, but it goes much further. Should someone have plastic surgery? If I want to kick somebody, I usually do not do it; a dog or a donkey cannot be trusted to behave so well. So should we return to "natural" manners, or is that not proper behavior? Is "natural food"—a big fad today—actually superior to other food? Is it unjust to pay double for organically grown produce?

Things are not necessarily better just because they are natural; a loaf of bread is better to eat than raw grain.[2] We can eat and digest sugar, though it may not be healthy for us; we can eat paper, but we cannot digest it. We may say that artificial sweetening is not good because it is not natural, but we can actually create artificial sweeteners out of a variety of materials; we can create cloth from oil; we can do the most bizarre things. Should we go "back to nature"? How far should we go? And if we do, why should we be vegetarians, like cows, and not carnivores, like tigers? Tigers, too, are a part of nature. Since we have choice, we have confusion.

These are questions not just for each individual human being, but for all of humanity. Some people have very clear-cut answers: everything natural—which means that which has not been changed or interfered with by man—is basically good, and those things that are not natural are evils that we humans have created. If we take a little philosophical jump back to the views of Rousseau, we see that idealizing nature is not a new idea. A number of educational systems were built according to these ideas. Even more so, some of the biggest political movements of our times were influenced by them.* Most of these attempts ended badly, even disastrously†—basically, because it seems that "nature" and "good" are not synonymous.

Even if we decide that we do want to return to nature, we cannot do it. Being both a part of nature and apart from nature, it is very difficult to determine what is natural for us, and what is unnatural. To complicate the problem further, humankind is distinct in not having any

*Strangely enough, both Communism and Nazism, different as they may be, are linked to the same source idea of returning to the primeval order; obviously, not with the same understanding of what that order is.
†If one prefers fiction, see for instance Lord of the Flies by William Golding, or the film based on it.

"natural" group to compare with. There are wild rats and domesticated ones, wild bulls and domesticated cows, but there are no "wild" human beings existing in a "natural state." Even the most primitive individuals and cultures are not a part of raw nature. Being human means that a great part of our existence is artificial, man-made.

With all that, we still have to be careful about our "mental ecology." We can draw some models and broad guidelines from nature about what can and should be done. However, we must remember that it is we who make those guidelines, that they are not written explicitly in red letters in nature. Furthermore, sometimes they can be abandoned, ignored, or changed. We should honor the patterns by which nature generally seems to function, but at the same time, we should take these rules with more than one grain of salt.

Moreover, using the general "laws of nature" as guidelines can be quite dangerous. Take, for instance, the Darwinian view of the world as "the survival of the fittest": it has been used in very ugly, vicious ways to justify killing (and even genocide), because "the fittest survive." That was not only morally very wrong, but it also showed how people can misunderstand a notion, turn it into a slogan—and then misuse it.

Furthermore, even if we decide to follow the "law of the jungle," it is not that simple. The jungle is complex; it has a myriad of different creatures that do not all behave alike. The mouse and the elephant both live in the wild, but behave differently. The amoebas and the cockroaches are very fit; they have existed longer than many other species. Should they be our models? The tyrannosaurus and the saber-toothed tiger have long been extinct, while squids and even earthworms have survived. Being able to chop off somebody's head is not a mark of superiority—not even in nature at its rawest.

What are the right models for our social life and our family life? This, too, is not an abstract question. What are our standards for deciding what is best? Nature provides so many models that the answer depends on who is defining the standards. Nature is too diverse, too strange, and offers too many choices to provide specific directives for human behavior. Given these caveats, we can look to nature for general guidelines, at least to determine when we are doing something that is very wrong.

The Talmud states, "Even if we were not given the Law, we could learn how to behave from the animals."[3] We would learn family life from the doves—they seem to be devoted to each other, they form permanent couples, and there are fewer divorces among them than among humans. They sometimes fight, they do not always behave like doves, but at least they do form permanent couples. We can learn sanitary behavior from the cats. They behave so very nicely—they cover everything neatly. However, even the models of the dove and the cat do not have labels saying that they are the right way for humans to behave. Maybe we should behave sexually like cats, and sanitarily like doves. That would be a different picture, but it would also be imitating nature.

Nature, then, is like a gigantic book. In that book there are many pages, each with different pictures, some of which are contradictory. We can always quote examples to prove whatever point we want to make, as people do from anthologies or books of quotations. Our freedom of choice gives us the ability to do everything, and our bond to nature compels us to use nature as a guideline, but also to make constant adaptations. When we read the pages of the book of nature, we need a commentary, because without one we get mixed up, we get lost in all the information that can be found there.

Yet, there are some advantages in consulting the book of nature. We may want to find out about our behavior, our emotions, our customs: are they just artifacts, temporary, man-made structures that will topple naturally if not held together by our willpower? When we find certain things that exist and flourish all around us, then we know that we are working with nature, and not against the general flow of nature. Of course we can, and do, express ourselves and behave in "unnatural" ways, but we know that they are bound to fall. A better understanding of the natural laws does not compel us to obey them, but we cannot ignore them. Watching nature can give us some notion about what is permanent and what is ephemeral, what is a promising path and what is a blind alley.

In this way, we will perceive that many grand moral and philosophical ideas are verbal restatements of things that exist all around us in nature. We cannot expect to hear nature express them in words, but they are there in other forms. It is as if we, who are endowed with the gift of speech, have to listen to others who can only use sign language. One should not look for the Ten Commandments on a fossil; yet they can be found enacted in animate and inanimate entities. This is true not only about very broad subjects, such as the importance of life, mutual aid, and the like; the idea of progress, for example, may sound very modern, but every seed growing into a tree proclaims it.

Watching nature may also help solve some problems and contemporary dilemmas. We can rely on book knowledge and journal ideology, but we can also derive some lessons about education from a cat teaching a kitten how to hunt; we can learn from birds about taking care of the young; from some animals, about sexual life; and from any social creature, about proper behavior during wartime. We may also learn about how precious life is, as well as about self-sacrifice.

We can therefore learn many important lessons from nature. We can see how certain noble and gracious things are done naturally—namely, without the interference of the special human ability to distort and change instincts. For example, when a maternal instinct is diverted toward a pet, when the instinct of self-preservation is subject to an ideology, or so many sensual deviations (e.g., bestiality). This does not mean, however, that we cannot search and find parallels also to the most atrocious things; in fact, it would be strange if there were none. If some deed or form of behavior has no natural counterpart, it may be just an abstract idea that can exist only in the mind but is impossible to realize because of inherent inconsistencies. If people do have the material and psychological ability to do something, there must somehow be a parallel to it in nonhuman nature.

However, finding some bizarre case does not turn such a behavior into a model for general conduct. There is a consensus, and there are general rules, and some even more general ones. These general rules that are found all around us should serve as guidance. Moving too far away from "raw" nature is not impossible, but should be taken as a warning. When we seek a path and find ourselves in a deserted place, this may be an indication that we have lost our way. Of course, this does not mean that the knowledgeable naturalist is always a better human being; a person may know what is right, and still decide not to act accordingly.

In a way, all of this can be summarized through a very old legend. When God created man, God said (Genesis 1:26), "Let us make man in our image, after our likeness." Traditionally, it is understood that God was speaking to the angels. If so, the plan was not very successful; we are not like angels. According to another interpretation, God was speaking to the whole of creation, to all of nature.[4] In that case, "Let us make man in our image" means, "Let each of you contribute something." The fox and the dove, the tiger and the sheep, the spider and the bee each contributed a small part—as did the angels and the devils.

We humans contain all the parts. Some of us are foxier than others, or more sheepish than others, but altogether, we contain all the traits found in nature. In that way, we are the sum total of nature, containing the macrocosm in our own microcosm.[5] Somehow, we have to learn from all our partners, and perhaps pray that the extra part—that "Divine spark" contributed by God—will help us make the right choices.

Good

⟜

I n the Middle Ages, Good was traditionally divided into three categories: the pleasant, the useful, and the moral. Indeed, to this day, we say that a person who is pleasing to the eye is "good-looking," or that certain foods "taste good." Useful things are also "good," although—like bitter medicine—they may not always be pleasant.

Each one of the various kinds of good—the aesthetic, the functional, and the moral—has a different set of rules with its own compelling inner logic, and unfortunately, the categories are not interconnected. Thus, beauty can be morally wrong, impractical, or even dangerous. Most poisonous mushrooms, for instance, are much more beautiful than the edible ones. Conversely, something that violates the laws of aesthetics is not necessarily immoral: an ugly person can be deeply righteous.

The first two kinds of good are relatively easy to define according to objective standards, and there are experts who can be consulted whenever questions arise about "goodness" in these particular meanings of the term. However, the third category, "moral good," is not as easily definable or measurable, nor are there many experts in this field—and those who do exist are seldom consulted. When we say that certain things are "obviously good" or "obviously evil," how do we know? Do we have an innate moral sense that guides us? If so, no exact site where it is located in the brain has as yet been found. Even if there were such a sense, to what extent could we rely on it?

The question of how we choose between good and evil is not just an abstract theoretical problem; we make moral choices many times each day. While many people can spend whole lifetimes without dealing with questions of aesthetics, and while we may hang on to useless things, or live without things that may be useful for us, we cannot ignore questions of good and evil. Whether alone or in society, active or passive, we have to make moral judgments all the time. Although there are very few people willing to announce publicly that they do not care about good and evil, many more act so tacitly. There are people who "cease to distinguish between good and evil, except for a slight inclination for the latter."[1] Such indifference—proclaimed by a number of politicians and "men of action"—is, itself, a clear choice. Ignoring the moral aspect of things is a vote for evil, not in the romantic tradition of Baudelaire's *Fleurs du Mal,* but in a very practical way.

Can we take law as our guide? Although many people

see law as the embodiment of moral good, law actually helps create and maintain social order. Nowadays, law does not even claim to address issues of morality, or good and evil. Most contemporary legal systems all over the world have ceased to believe in any "natural law" that may even claim to represent good and morality. Lawmakers in various countries still do—out of habit, or for political considerations—make noises to the effect that the legal system is closely connected with morality, but the fact is that legal systems basically care for their own internal consistency, and for reflecting the moods and desires of the population.

In fact, life is full of evil things that law does not even address, either because it is not interested in them, or because it cannot really touch them. Many aspects of human behavior, from financial transactions to personal conduct, are legal while being immoral to a lesser or greater degree. One can be offensive and rude, and make everybody unhappy, and still act in a perfectly legal way. We cannot, then, rely on the law as a guideline for moral good.

Many of us believe in, or have experienced, an inner "thin small voice" (1 Kings 19:12), telling us what is good and what is evil. But this seemingly innate inner voice is, in fact, conditioned by time, place, and culture, as well as by personal taste. We are living in a very noisy culture that bombards us with books, magazines, newspapers, radio, television, movies, and video games—a multitude of voices trying to guide, advise, influence, or convince us. These voices implant ideas in us, which we often repeat without thinking. Even when we think that we are making our own statements, we may merely be repeating the words of a TV announcer we heard some time before. We often do not verify what we hear, yet we believe it, adhere to it, and use it. It is practically impossible to differentiate between true feeling and external noise.

Even in less noisy times, people did not live in isolation. Outside influences begin with one's parents, and then expand to include friends and society. Even in the smallest society, there are people of influence whose opinions are assimilated by the individual. Beyond that, personal involvement inevitably clouds our moral judgment. Personal involvement means that we tend to justify our actions, even when we know that we are wrong; we fortify ourselves with arguments, and then upholster them with more arguments, to convince ourselves, and others, that we did right.[2] This is not just a modern, skeptical idea: King Solomon already said, "All the ways of man are clear in his eyes."[3] For all these reasons, our "common sense," our innate reaction, is actually reliable in only a very small number of cases, usually the less important ones.

In small societies, there is a consensus as to what is morally right or wrong, which dictates clear and unambiguous rules of behavior. The larger and more heterogeneous a society is, the more confusing are one's moral decisions, because every subgroup has its rights and wrongs. According to anthropological and sociological research, there is hardly one thing that is considered immoral all around the world. Similarly, we can find almost nothing that is universally considered good. Very often, the laws of social consensus are not written, or even explicitly formulated, and although people abide by them, they may be unaware of the fact that the things they are doing, or abstaining from, are based on moral rules.

Therefore, as people from various cultures meet each other and search for a common moral ground, they discover moral relativism; rules that seem perfectly normal, even obvious, in one society may seem completely bizarre in another. For instance, most societies do not approve of cannibalism; on the other hand, there were societies in which it was practiced publicly and ceremoniously. Our disapproval of cannibalism surely does not stem from practical reasons. Our disapproval of cannibalism may be based on moral reasons, but it could very well be that it is abhorrent to us because it transgresses our sense of the aesthetics of behavior.

To add to the confusion, actions that are considered completely immoral in one place or time, or in one set of circumstances, are not considered so reprehensible when the situation changes. Thus, even rules about clearly moral issues, such as murder, depend not only on the norms of a particular society, but also on the conditions in a society at a particular moment. In a country at war, people are trained to kill; one can call it by nicer names, but in fact, it is legally approved murder, which is often morally sanctioned also.[4] To give what may seem a trivial example: during the Second World War, when a blackout was mandatory, children grew up understanding that no lights must be seen from the outside. Once the war was over, children who saw their parents open the shutters at night were shocked by their "immorality."

Does this mean that good and evil are totally relative, and, therefore, that everything is acceptable? Are there any meta-moral laws? For example, can an entire society or a whole era be wrong?

A case in point is the Nuremberg trials. In these trials, Nazi leaders were judged as war criminals. However, according to the laws of Nazi Germany, these crimes were fully legal acts, done in obedience to laws that were decreed and approved in a perfectly democratic way.* The underlying premise of these trials was that some acts are illegal, even if the law—at least the local law—allows them, because they violate a fundamental, universally binding human morality that is beyond local law, beyond the realm of approved authority, social norms, ideology, and propaganda.

What was not clarified at the Nuremberg trials, and may never be clarified, is the question of how we derive those higher laws. What moral absolutes apply when nobody can be trusted—when the army commander and the courtroom judge are legally right, socially approved, but evil?

If we believe in God, then we connect our standards of

*This also goes to show, by the way, that democracy is not a safeguard against immorality.

good with God. These standards, however, are not always internalized; more often than not, people act according to them because the "policeman" is watching, and not because they deem those acts intrinsically right or wrong. My great-grandfather, who was a Hassidic Rebbe, was once driving along a country road. The coachman saw an apple orchard, jumped out, and began to take some apples. The Rebbe cried out, "You are being watched! You are being watched!" The coachman did not linger a second—he jumped back in the carriage and drove the horses as fast as he could. After a while, when they were a considerable distance away, he stopped and said, "But I did not see anybody watching!" The Rebbe replied, "God is watching you."

Even if we do not believe, we may still have a set of absolute values. In order to be meaningful, these absolutes have to go beyond the subjective and ephemeral feelings of the individual. Even if we do not believe in Divine revelation, at least we can use cross-cultural comparison to find out what those fundamental values are.

The notion that some general structure of values is a common denominator for all groups and societies is based on natural and theological considerations. In the common root of all humanity (Adam and Eve, if you wish), there should be some parts that are still in agreement, however much they may have diverged due to time and circumstances. It is so in external form: although races differ in size and shape, in color and detail, there are still enough common elements to unify the human species. The same is true about psychological elements, skills, and abilities that all humans—even from very different cultures— share. Thus, even when a particular society has not created a certain skill—writing, for example—when individuals of that society move to a literate society, they are easily able to acquire that skill. Basic moral norms, too, are connected with the basic makeup of humanity. They may happen to have developed differently in some societies, or even be lacking in others, but they are found within. When societies are carefully examined, and generalizations are made, these moral norms can create a sustainable system that will make sense and be acceptable to all.

Philosophers, sages, prophets, and scholars, Jewish and non-Jewish alike, have searched for and tried to formulate moral absolutes, the ethical rules about good and evil that should govern our behavior.

The prophet Micah (6:8), for instance, formulates three fundamental principles: "He [God] has shown you, O man, what is good; and what does the Lord require from you? To act justly and to love mercy and to walk humbly with your God." The Talmud says these three dicta contain all of the Biblical commandments within them.[5] At a later period, a Gentile once came to Hillel the Elder[6] asking to be taught the whole law "on one leg." This ambiguous phrase may mean either that he wanted to be taught everything while actually standing on one leg, or that he was asking Hillel to define one guiding principle—"leg"—that underlies the whole Torah. Hillel answered with the epigrammatic statement, "What you hate to have done unto you, do not do to others."[7] Later commentators add that this dictum applies not only to social interactions, but also to our dealings with God; we have to behave toward God in the same way that we want God to behave toward us.[8] Much later, the German philosopher Kant defined morality, the basic law of ethics, as "that which is equally good for everybody."[9]

We tend to expect moral laws to give clear answers, but in fact, attempts to formulate moral universals are inherently incomplete. Broad-spectrum definitions of good do not provide black-and-white, yes-or-no answers. For one thing, people have their idiosyncrasies, their special tastes and their preferences, even in the realm of good and morality. Moreover, in moral issues, it is only very seldom that we have to choose between black and white, between the clearly good and the clearly evil. In most cases, the choices that we face are between shades of gray, namely, between a lesser good and a greater good, a lesser evil and a greater evil.

Universal moral laws are generalizations, and as such, they cannot possibly cover all the specifics. Real judgments take many factors into consideration. In order to function as a guide for human behavior, grand statements must be supported by a code of law or a system of ethics that works out the details. This cannot be left to a whim, or a vague, obscure, and undefined sense or feeling about right and wrong.

In the search for good, the first step is to throw away

the trash—the cultural noise, the ephemeral points of view. Beyond that noise, the next step is to build a scale of values, a viable and stable order of priorities and gradations of good and evil that will be capable of standing on its own, regardless of geography or history. Such an order of priorities is essential for coping with clashes between values.

Let's take a very simple example: most people will agree that in most cases, murder is evil. Yet there is also consensus that self-defense overrides the commandment not to kill (Exodus 20:13). Is self-preservation always the supreme good? Are there no limits to self-preservation? Are there things that are worse than death? Are there principles that are worth killing or dying for?

The seven commandments given to the children of Noah[10] are such a basic set of laws that deal with good and evil—not from an interpersonal or social point of view, but rather, aiming for absolute values. They attempt to delineate the minimal moral prerequisites for humanity. In Jewish law, the *Halakhah,* there is an elaborate, highly detailed scale of values that establishes orders of priorities in a great variety of cases and situations.

Whatever the moral system may be, it must be consistent and have an inner harmony, with all its parts working together smoothly. This inner harmony is, in fact, the common denominator for all the types of good. Just as all the parts of a practical object should work together smoothly, and a beautiful object has to have inner harmony, so, too, moral good cannot exist as separate, discrete dicta that do not relate to each other harmoniously. Once we have such a scale of values and priorities, we can make judgments; there will be things that we will accept and things we will reject, things that will have supreme value and others that will carry lesser weight.

Take bridges as an example: individual bridges can differ greatly from each other in their structure, purpose, and materials; still, there are some universal laws of bridge building. Every bridge has to span a gap, and should be structured to sustain the weight it is expected to hold. These two criteria encompass an enormous number of details, which give rise to the great variations in the way bridges are built, and how they look. However, because of the common interplay of physical laws and human needs, there is, at the basis of their functional elements, a certain uniformity, and even an aesthetic value to all of them.

Moral codes, too, may differ considerably from each other. They must also have structural integrity, in order to sustain the burden—namely, the clash between values—and span the gap between the material and the spiritual, the earthly and the divine. The search for a moral system should extend in three directions: it should be wide enough to encompass the vast range of human behavior; long enough to include past, present, and future; and high enough to be a bridge to Heaven.

These "dimensions" of morality are not merely poetical expressions; they are guidelines that can be used in the search for good. The first guideline is the generality of the rules. When a code covers only a limited part of life, it may be useful as a practical civil law, or, in other cases, as a manual for rituals, but the fact that it is limited means that it cannot be a moral law. At best, it can serve as a small part of one.

The book of law may tell one what to do about contracts and torts, but not about cursing somebody in one's heart, or about how to treat a child who did not do his homework. One may get exact information about every detail of a ritual, and yet know nothing about causing mental suffering.

The same fault is also apparent when applying a moral code to different places and different people. Some moral statements will be valid within an affluent civilized society, but will make no sense in a poor, war-torn country. The same is true in regard to time. Is certain moral advice suitable only for a defined period within our life span? Does the idea apply to the very young or the very old? In a broader sense, could the same law be valid for decades, or for six hundred years? If a certain measure of good and evil is dated, it will shortly be outdated.

Regarding the dimension of height (or depth, whatever way we choose to define it), some codes of moral behavior are just flat. They do not deal with deeper, more intense self-searching. It may be right to behave in a certain way, but it is also a pity that one is satisfied with that level of morality. Behaving in a neighborly way, not treading on the grass, and paying taxes are all nice things, but what about sacrificing something precious in order to save a life? Morality that does not have anything of the sublime in it may be very convenient and "normal," but it is dangerously close to total indifference, to the corruption of death.

In an ancient book about morals, there is a dispute: "[One who says] 'Mine is mine and yours is yours' is the average person; some say that is the quality of the city of Sodom."[11] A flat, legal-like form of morality may also be a prelude to extreme vice. In the realm of good, people who do not have a Heaven above their heads may find that they also do not possess a soil to walk upon.

Is such a multidimensional good easy to achieve? Perhaps it is not; but the search for it may create better people.

Spirit and Matter

✦

We human beings are amphibians. We are not like frogs, but we *are* amphibious. We live in two worlds: the material and the spiritual, and sometimes on the borderline between them. We are aware of the differences, just as the difference between dry land and water is clear even to the smallest frog. However, although we jump continuously from one existence to the other, we are often unaware of the jump. Although we live in two worlds, one of them seems to be the real world, the real existence, while the other seems much more hazy, not quite as real.

The material world is obvious. We have material bodies, and we go about living our lives within the world of matter. With all our senses, we can perceive directly only aspects of that material world. We tend to feel that the material life we live is the "real" existence—True Reality. We smell scents and hear sounds, and our sense of sight is our main way of understanding the world, but the ultimate way in which we verify the existence of things is by touching them. We equate real with tangible. Things that we cannot grasp in our hands are less real to us. Although we know—either from books or from direct experience—that most things, even in the physical-material world, cannot be perceived through our senses (from radioactive rays to microscopic germs), still, this does not change our strong, primitive notion that reality is that which we can sense. Because we can touch it, the material world is real.

In a different way, we are also participants in another, nonmaterial world. This abstract, nontangible world is certainly not in the same category of reality, yet it is no less real. Just as we inhabit the material world, we also exist in a spiritual world. Unfortunately, the word "spiritual" has acquired mystical and supernatural connotations, and is used too frequently by all kinds of unreliable people, from bleary-eyed old ladies speaking about spirituality to quacks selling spiritual medicines and spiritual workshops that will make us wise, beautiful, successful, and thin. Since such "spirituality" seems to range from wishy-washy to clinically crazy, it is not at all astonishing that some people keep a safe distance.

The spiritual world we live in is very close and real. It is not the realm of ghosts and disembodied beings, where powers and vibrations (whatever they are) roam. The spiritual world is, first and foremost, all the things we relate

to through our minds. This includes our thoughts and
emotions, love, hate, and envy, the ability to read, to enjoy music, or to solve equations, to know that we exist,
and to relate to others. All these are intangible—they cannot be touched or weighed. However, they are commonplace, direct experiences, and they are as real as anything
can be. All these together make up our second world, the
spiritual one.

Actually, the notions of spirit and matter are very simple; there is nothing startling or exceptional about them.
We are material and spiritual. Our existence is a double
existence: on one side, a body with senses that perceive
matter; on the other, the spirit that conceives thinking
and emotional processes—two worlds running parallel,
with varying emphasis on each at different times. In some
sense, we are more than just a simple amphibian, jumping from one environment into the other. We do something far more complex: we live in two different existences
simultaneously. We live in one with our bodies, and in another through our minds, and the two of them mingle all
the time.

Our assumption that existence is primarily physical,
and that reality is that which is tangible, is not self-evident, natural, or inborn. This sort of thinking (a spiritual
phenomenon in itself) is based on cultural maxims that
are taught to us. From a very young age, we are taught
that dreams, ideas, and thoughts are not real, and that
what we say, think, and dream do not count. In turn, we
transmit to our children—not always in words—the no-

tion that "reality" is that which can be seen and touched. Our children get the message continuously, in both subtle and not so subtle ways: "If it does not exist in matter, it does not matter." In our culture, if a small child breaks a cup, we scold him; if he cuts his finger, we are worried; but if a child speaks of his dreams and imaginations, we dismiss them as unimportant, and even more—as unreal.

In this way, we are unintentionally, but continuously, brainwashed into thinking that the spiritual is not very real, and therefore we discount it in many ways. This education has many evolutionary advantages, mostly to cats, cattle, or apes, who have to rely on their senses and not on their thoughts (if they have any). Whether it is helpful in the long run for human beings is quite doubtful. When we ignore or discount the intangible, we are misleading ourselves. If spirituality were only pondering about angels, we could ignore it, claiming that angels are of no interest to us. As things are, we cannot ignore or rid ourselves of the spiritual aspect of our life, so long as we are conscious.

What is that spiritual aspect? Religious and philosophical ideas are part of the realm of the spirit, but they are not what define it. "Spiritual" encompasses many things, some of which have practical, material manifestations that are clearly the end product of a spiritual process. The mathematician and the writer, the creative artist or the person who curses, are all connected to the spiritual realm. Spirituality refers to a nonmaterial reality that is grasped by a different form of sensor. It is a matter of inner perception rather than outer sensation; it is our inner world. Being conscious, understanding and measuring, planning and calculating, as well as loving and hating, are all parts of our spiritual being.

All of this has nothing to do with an idealistic (as opposed to materialistic) philosophy. If one wants, one may claim that all mental activity is just a result of chemical and electrical reactions in the brain cells. The same is equally true of our sensory perception, and it does not invalidate the existence of an objective world. The mental process may create a number of unreal things—such as dreams or calculation mistakes—in the same way that our senses can be misleading. We are always checking and correlating our sensory observations. We learn, for example, that the little man seen at a distance does not objectively become bigger as we come closer to him.

The fact that the spiritual world is perceived only inside the brain, and not otherwise, is the same as the fact that we cannot see with our noses or hands. It is true that we get to the spiritual world through an electrochemical function of complex nerve cells. As Henri Bergson observed, the fact that a dress is on a hanger, and will move as the hanger moves, and even fall with it, does not mean that the hanger is superior, and surely not that the hanger and the dress are identical. Is the spiritual world real? It is, in the same way that everything which exists is real. It cannot be touched, just as a scent or a magnetic field cannot be touched; it cannot be seen, just as the sound of a trumpet is invisible. Yet it can be perceived and measured, checked and defined by its own tools of perception and measurement.

Some of us have been taught in school that thinking is a serious, orderly process, done by following certain rules and regulations. It should, however, be remembered that as long as we are doing any thinking, we are in the realm of the spiritual. We can think about right things or wrong things, about high, beautiful things, or about low and degrading things. We may think about things of no importance, we may have idle dreams or idle thoughts, but we cannot stop thinking. To stop the process of thinking, to stop our spiritual existence, is as hard, or even harder, than stopping our material existence. As long as the physical body is functioning, we cannot stop thinking. Our two worlds are so intertwined that it is practically impossible for us, at least while we are conscious, to be in one world without being in the other as well.

All those things that are not tangible are "spiritual," and that includes most of our "self": what we are, what we think, what we dream, what we feel. None of this is real in the material sense; it is all part of what we call the spiritual realm. This spiritual world exists not just for very "spiritual" people, but for everybody.

When people talk to each other, physically they are emitting sound waves, which are not inherently meaningful in any way. Internally, they may be trying to merge their spiritual experiences, opening their worlds to each other. When I tell someone about myself, I open to the other a new nonmaterial existence, one the other has never visited before. These things are done by everyone who communicates. Though the communication is

achieved through physical means, in our physical existence, the meaning of the communication is a nonphysical reality. The actions of speaking, writing, and signaling
are the physical means of communication, while the content is the spiritual part.

Citizenship and loyalty, group membership and alien-
ation, are all nonmaterial things. We make and break
spiritual relationships all the time, although we are not
accustomed to speaking about these as "spiritual" acts. In
most cases, the material aspect is usually the unimportant part of our relationships. Although we do not usually
think of it as such, a business partnership is a spiritual
agreement, not a material bond. When two people shake
hands, what they do with their hands is not the important
part of the relationship. The more intimate the relationship, the more important the role of the spiritual side relative to the material side.

Love is surely not a material thing. The relationship
between people who love each other is not material. It
may have many material manifestations, but the feeling,
the emotion itself, is entirely spiritual. Family is also
based only on nonmaterial reality. We can point a finger at
particular bodies, yet the relationship with them is not
based on how physically close or distant we are, or on biological proof, but rather on what we feel about them.

In the same way, envy, hatred, joy, and all our other
emotions are not material things, although they may relate to a material object. The people that we love and the
people that we hate have their own material realities, but

the love and the hate are part of our amphibian existence.

When a person is successful in any way, what does that really mean? Usually, it is not a physical reality. Being successful, being "on top," is not best measured by a physical yardstick. It is a spiritual relationship or connection in which the successful person is acknowledged by others as being successful. The same is true of power—a powerful person is not necessarily a fellow who can lift three hundred pounds. The power of a commander, of a politician, or of a leader is spiritual, not material. Even something as quantifiable as money is in many ways not material. It is not just the physical money that constitutes wealth; it is also the notion of possession, as well as our agreement that money is a symbol for other things.

In the simplest sense of the word, then, everybody is both physical and spiritual. Our dual citizenship is inherent in us. It is not a matter of choosing between the two worlds; we really cannot make such a choice. Instead, we are confronted with a simpler, yet more challenging choice— each person must choose at what level to be spiritual. Without entering into a deep philosophical discussion, we can ask whether we are primarily material beings with a part immersed in a spiritual existence, or spiritual beings with a part rooted in the four-dimensional physical world. We have to choose what kind of spiritual existence we want.

In the physical world, we can choose where we dwell. I can choose to live in the cellar all my life, or I can live in the upper stories. I can live in a town or in a village; that is a matter of choice or chance. We have the same ability to move within our other world, the spiritual world. We actually have more freedom both for ourselves and vis-à-vis others than in the material world. Our inner reality contains a whole universe, which is—almost by definition—much bigger than the other, material one. I cannot always enlarge my physical boundaries, and the laws that apply to physical objects are far more fixed and inflexible than the laws that apply to spiritual entities.

If I want to hurt someone else, I am limited both by law and by my physical ability. I have far more leeway to curse than to do physical damage. Many aspects of our material existence are not under our control or subject to our volition. Often we are compelled by external circumstances to live in one place rather than another. We are born in a certain place; moving from one place to another is not always easy. To walk to the next town may take hours; to go to the next galaxy in one's mind takes an instant. In fact, I do not even have to move much in order to do this kind of roaming. Like it or not, we are citizens of the spiritual world, but where we dwell within it is our decision. Just as I can put my physical body into a garden of wonderful scents or into a stinking sewer, the same is true in the spiritual world. We each choose whether our lives will be a detective novel, a scandal sheet, or a scripture.

Of course, just as there are limits to our physical choices, there are limits to our spiritual choices. In the spiritual realm, too, we are pushed, or forced by necessity to dwell in a particular region. For instance, in school, whether we want to or not, we are forced into the intellectual realm of reading, which is, strange as it may seem, the process of translating physical symbols into spiritual understanding. Similarly, just as we do not like to be forced to live in certain places, some of us do not like to be compelled to do mathematics.

Time is an unavoidable limit, and therefore we have to decide what to do with the time available. I may want to be everywhere at once; practically, I cannot do so. I have to choose whether I want to visit Nepal or I want to travel to Israel; I cannot be in both places at the same time. It is the same with spiritual choices—most of us cannot think about two things simultaneously, so we have to choose.

Lack of education is another form of handicap. If I do not know a language, I cannot read that language. If I have not learned mathematics, I cannot balance my checkbook.

To use a more vivid image, some people are born handicapped, blind, deaf, or without a sense of smell. Some people suffer from the same type of handicap in the spiritual realm—they are forced to live a limited spiritual life by a mental inability to grasp spiritual realities. There are realms that require some special talent. Certain spiritual realms may be closed to a person who does not have the requisite special ability. A person may have the spiritual ability to hear and enjoy music, but not the spiritual ability to compose or perform it. In that sense, that person is spiritually handicapped in that realm.

These are actual limits, as real as if they were physical limits. Some of them can be overcome; some of them cannot be overcome, at least in this lifetime. Within the constraints of these limitations, we make choices about our spiritual life. People may decide, for many frivolous reasons, to sever part of their sensory connection to the physical world; one can choose to put out one's eyes, to make oneself deaf, or to maim oneself in other ways. In the spiritual realm, too, a person may decide not to think about certain matters, not to deal with certain subjects, or not to be interested in them. In this way, whether intentionally or not, we make ourselves spiritually blind and deaf, and handicap ourselves in that realm.

In the spiritual world, people can demean themselves from the level of full human capacity to a level comparable to animal life, or even lower. A person may go through life in a body that is clearly human, yet have the internal, spiritual life of a horse, pulling the cart of his life, eating and defecating, having sex and sleeping, living in the physical realm; there is not much difference between the person and the horse, other than the external form. They have basically the same dreams, the same desires, and live in somewhat the same world.

A chicken may spend her whole life cooped in a small cage; she is fed there, she lays her eggs there, she may even be slaughtered there. We may pity her, but it is possible that if this chicken could express her mind, she would not complain too bitterly. It may be a safe, quiet life without too much worry and stress. We may live the same kind of life, spiritually speaking, and may not feel that anything is missing.

This is not a question of good and evil; it is, rather, a matter of being degraded or being elevated. To give an extreme example, we often pity people who are physically handicapped. We feel deeper pity when we see people who are mentally handicapped. When we see a retarded child, we feel pity, but not for the child's subjective state—a mentally handicapped child may be as happy as any other child, maybe even happier. We feel sad about the lack of development of the human potential. When a person is in a coma, we feel a deep sense of pity, not because that person is suffering, but because that condition is a degradation of someone who once could act, and now cannot. The spiritual degradation of working far below capacity should engender the same feeling of pity. A human being has a huge spiritual potential; when such a creature lives life at a much lower level, it is not sinful—it is just a pity.

If I am capable of moving around but I am confined, then I feel deprived. If I am capable of soaring to heaven but I crawl on the floor, then I am confined. It is a very unfortunate person who is compelled to live such an impoverished life. This form of poverty has nothing to do with material circumstances, nor does it correlate with a feeling of satisfaction. One person may live a very exciting spiritual life, yet not be satisfied. Conversely, an impoverished way of life can be subjectively quite satisfying, especially if the person does not know any better, or does not know about the ability to choose.

If there were any valid spiritual measurement, it would measure the discrepancy between one's ability as a human being and one's performance in life. The basic definition of physical health and well-being is very simple: a body in which all the parts are functioning to capacity. The same definition applies in the other realm of existence. A person is complete when his or her achievement is appropriate to his or her capacity.

Growing spiritually means that I can now do more with my mind than I could do before. Our amphibious creature has to make a declaration of independence, like freeing a slave. This creature has the freedom to move, and that freedom does not require anything extraordinary or unattainable or depend on any special holiness. Moving requires knowing that the possibility to move exists, finding out what one's abilities and capacity are, and renewing the relationship between body and spirit.

We tend to shy away from spirituality—it is too big to encompass, and we are afraid of its vast size. If you put a small creature in a big room, the creature becomes frightened, cowers in a corner, and does not want to explore the larger space. In the same way, we allow ourselves to live in a confined place, and we get accustomed to operating in a limited way.

Whenever we open a new space, whether it is a new room or a new country, outer space or inner space, the opportunity arises for strife or for cooperation. Any new relationship requires conscious choice. We can decide whether it will be a relationship of animosity, of friendship, or of neutrality. Usually, if we do not want to be too embarrassed, we try to maintain strict neutrality, in the same way that we do not collide with people physically.

We choose the quality of our relationship with the spiritual world. We can choose whether to deal with practical things that may be useful for our life plan, to focus on abstract intellectual ideas, or to devote ourselves to acts of kindness. Any of these choices would enlarge a person's spiritual borders. One person would grow functionally, one intellectually, the third one in empathy. Any one of these choices would utilize the person's spiritual side. A person who is pure intellect and a person who is full of empathy and benevolence are both enlarging themselves spiritually. Deciding who is superior, the intellectual or the saint, is a different discussion. We are speaking here about spirit, not about goodness or saintliness. Each realm of growth will be measured on a different scale—by its influence on society, by its saintliness, or simply by how the person feels about himself.

Spirituality and spiritual entities are not inherently superior or better than material ones. Good and evil can both be spiritual or physical. Although some religious groups tend to equate spiritual with good, matter and body with evil,* it is obviously untrue. There can be extremely evil spiritual worlds, from Nazi ideology to everyday cruelty. Avarice and hatred are spiritual qualities, but surely not good ones. The body, too, may become a vehicle

*This is a rather ancient idea, best developed in the Manichaean religion, which had a strong influence on some other religions, and some extreme manifestations in numerous sects—e.g., the Cathars and the Albigenses of the Middle Ages, as well as some groups in more recent times.

for all kinds of evil, just because the spirit within it is evil. However, it, too, can be, both in itself and as a tool, a means to very admirable things. A great philosopher is not inherently superior to the long-distance runner, although societies may differ in favoring one or the other. Likewise, in Heaven they will be judged according to their attitude to holiness, rather than according to their mental or physical prowess.

Our dual relationship to the physical and the spiritual worlds exists. Whether we want it or not, we cannot avoid either world. What we can do is develop a clearer understanding of how we function, and define what is important to us. Had we infinite time to spend, we could do anything and everything. Since our time in the physical world is limited, it is crucial that we refine our standards, and focus on the important things, even if they cannot be defined in a tangible way. It is essential to ask what really counts.

It is a pity that as children, we acquire confused notions about matter and spirit. We will remain confused as adults—unless we define these words by their simple, proper meanings. It is up to us to define our perception of these worlds properly, so that we can make our decisions rightly, and perhaps also enable our children to receive a different, better message. Perhaps, then, they will become different people, and create a different world for themselves. When we recognize matter as matter, and spirit as spirit, then we find both worlds open before us, and this amphibious creature will be able to achieve its maximum potential in each realm.

Faith

❧

For many people, among them those who either regret or boast about their being nonbelievers, the word "Faith," written with a very capital F, is a very big block. In reality, however, faith is related not only to Great Things; it has to do just as much, if not more, with the myriad of little things that are a part of everybody's daily life.

There are, obviously, many people who are credulous, and some others who are much less so, but nearly everyone is a believer to some degree. Belief exists even in the most hardheaded, rational nonbelievers. Many of us take pride in our rationality—we think we base our actions and thoughts on accurate knowledge, verified facts, and an orderly sorting and sifting of opinions. The truth, however, is that nobody is a total nonbeliever; all of us accept almost everything on faith.

Faith, in the everyday, common sense of the word, is so ingrained in our lives that we cannot do anything without it. We accept what we are taught in school and what we learn in the street. Most of these things are not only un-verified, they are unverifiable, yet they are still a huge part of our lives. It is practically impossible to do any real checking about most basic things. We do not have the time, the facilities, or the talents to find out for ourselves about most things that we say we know. We accept the facts about the height of Mount Everest—even most of the people who climb it do not bother to double-check the measurements—just as we accept facts about cars and electricity, signing contracts, and walking in the street. We take so much for granted because we have faith—to some degree—in the car dealer and the electrician, and in the normal, even decent, behavior of those people we en-counter.

What we perceive as the dichotomy between "matters of faith" and "indisputable facts" has less to do with ra-tionality than with what is socially accepted within our particular society, social group, and historical era. What "everybody knows" is something that we do not feel obli-gated to prove for ourselves. For the same reason, those things that are not a part of our accepted wisdom are left to the believer.

A microbiologist who did research in Africa used a very bright young local boy to run errands. He once tried to ex-plain his research to the boy, describing the very tiny, in-visible microbes that are all over the room, adding that they are liable to make a person ill, or even to kill him. To that, the child, who was educated by missionaries, retorted, "But sir, we Christians surely do not believe in that!" In some places, the existence of devils is an accepted fact, and everyone knows for sure that they exist; in other places, for the same frivolous reasons, no one believes in them. Thus, while our sets of belief are contextual, the underlying nature of faith is the same all around the world.

A crisis of faith, whether personal or general, is the result of cultural changes, both large and small. It is a matter of luck, of course, in what age one is born. There are ages in which faith is à la mode, and ages in which it is not fashionable to be a believer. Cultural fashions change no less than those of clothing. Just as there are fashion designers who set the style for women's dresses and men's ties, there are also people who create the intellectual fashion of the times, and decide what people should and should not believe. Yet, while we know who makes the rules about women's dresses, we usually do not know who is behind the intellectual fashions.*

In the last thirty years, the Nobel Prize for literature has not had literary significance; it has been a forum for political statements of various sorts. Those who distribute the prizes probably have slide rules to calculate who is the up-and-coming person to get the prize: a man, a woman, black, white, oppressed, more oppressed, even more oppressed. Even in those times when prizes were given for purely literary reasons, the list contained some great writers, alongside others whom no-

In an age of faith, people do not air their doubts and misgivings; most of them will never even have any doubts, because it is the social norm to believe. In other eras, it is just the opposite: skepticism is fashionable, and everyone joins in, following the admonition of the proverbial modern mother, "Why can't you be a nonconformist, like everybody else?" Thus, everyone adheres to an idea that seems understandable and reasonable in their period in history; later, people may look back and wonder how they could possibly have held such an absurd belief.

For instance, not so long ago, in "the Red decades" of European and American history, it was commonly thought that everyone of any account was a Communist, or at least a sympathizer—including intellectuals, trendsetters, people who should have known better, and people who should have been far more critical. It was a period in which people were obstinate believers, persisting in their belief and ignoring any evidence to the contrary. Then the fad passed; now, believing in Communism seems out of step with the times. For the same wrong reasons that people once believed, they now have ceased to believe. Nothing intrinsic has changed—only the fashion shifted.

Cultural fashions influence not only opinions about art, morality, and politics, they affect almost every facet of

body remembers. At the time that they received the prize, they were all at the peak of their fame; now, it is difficult to imagine why anyone saw any value in their work, though it may have set the intellectual trends of the day.

life. Fashion creates things that people buy, wear, use, and hang on the walls, and we are trained not only to buy them, but also to enjoy them. The same law of fashion also changes our outlook and attitude about matters that seem to be merely utilitarian. From furniture to architecture, things are chosen not because it is sensible to do so, but because they are fashionable. Think, for instance, how bizarre and unnatural skyscrapers look. There may be good reasons why they are built in certain places or in certain ways; in others, they make no sense at all. We build huge glass structures in order to let the light in, and then we fill those structures with curtains, to block the light. Since glass buildings have become fashionable, we have glass buildings, even though they are neither useful nor beautiful.

In our times, the cultural rules allow for a certain amount of freedom—although quite limited—in our choice of what we consider to be beautiful. In other periods, society was more decisive. There would not even be disputes about beauty, since there was only one acceptable style, and all other styles were unacceptable. In ancient Egyptian paintings, all the faces are in profile, regardless of the stance of the body. If we did not know better, we would think that the Egyptians just did not know how to draw; they were too primitive. However, their drawings of animals are very realistic—only the human beings look stiff and unnatural. When Egyptian artists were allowed to make natural drawings, they were very good at it.[1] Apparently, certain poses were just a fashion of art, and those poor artists were obligated to depict people according to the convention.

This adherence to fashion can also be found in architecture. There are no arches in ancient Egyptian buildings. It seems strange that people who were quite technologically advanced would not utilize such a functional structure. As it turns out, the Egyptians did know about arches, but they used them for sewage canals; they thought it beneath their dignity to construct dwellings with arches. It was not the fashion, so it did not exist.

Cultural fashion—or, as it has been called, "the spirit of the times"—has such tremendous power that it not only influences philosophy, beauty, and the like; even modern exact sciences are under its rule. In all sciences, including mathematics, there are periods in which certain questions become important and tempting, followed by periods in which these same subjects or methods lie dormant, until a new period comes. For example, the furious growth of physics—especially atomic and subatomic physics—in the first half of the twentieth century, compared to its development in the second half of this century; the enormous growth of biology, biochemistry, and biophysics in the second half of this century; the recent flourishing—in popular interest, as well as in scientific work—of ecology; the ups and downs of space research; or the changes of interest and development in synthetic geometry versus analytical geometry. Many books have tried to explain these changes, and why they happen in the ways they do. However, all these explanations—regardless of whether they are right or wrong—do not contradict the most obvious fact: the change itself.

The decades or centuries of belief come and go, to be replaced by periods of skepticism or indifference, and then, by a profound change in the attitude toward faith. In an age of faith, it is easy to believe. In fact, in such an age, faith does not even require any belief. In certain times and places, one could not even speak about belief in God; it was a simple, self-evident fact. Not believing in God was a little more bizarre than doubting that the earth is round.

Generally, we accept the dictates of society almost without noticing. We take things for granted, we jump to conclusions, and we accept common knowledge and everyday realities unchallenged. None but the most abstract philosopher would doubt the existence of his own nose. However, when it comes to Faith with a capital F, things become more difficult; many people just cannot accept it.

Our times are clearly different. Our fin de siècle is not an age of Faith. Incidentally, we are not in an age of rationality or skepticism either, but rather in a time of credulity. We do indeed believe, or half-believe, in thousands of things—some of them pure nonsense—but not in Faith, in the capital F sense. There is a Jewish anecdote about two students who went for a walk in the woods, and happened to be in the line of fire of a hunter. When the shots whizzed over their heads, they were frightened and fell down, imagining that they were hit. After some time, one of them raised his head cautiously, saying, "It seems that we are still alive." To which his friend responded, "And what is the basis for this assumption?" Surely, most people would not go that far.

The difference between the two levels of faith—faith in conventional wisdom, and faith in God—is not grounded in any psychological disparity, but rather in societal norms. When a person says that he is a nonbeliever, it is not a very accurate statement. A real nonbeliever would not get out of bed. If he did get out of bed, he would not take a step, because almost everything that we do depends on hundreds or thousands of beliefs, from believing that the sun will rise tomorrow to believing that salt is still salty.

Organized religions dictate the doctrines of faith that people are to believe; at the same time, they also set out what is heretical, what is not to be believed. When organized religion went out of style, and its nineteenth-century substitute, science, became far less dogmatic and self-assured,* that opened the way for superstition. Especially for the intellectuals and pseudo-intellectuals, this was not a mishap, but a rather natural consequence.

A true agnostic is actually open to belief in every possible faith or superstition, because nothing is completely impossible, and there are no prescribed or proscribed beliefs. Thus, he is fair game for every movement, every "ism," and every possibility. Everything is possible for a

*The theory of relativity, quantum mechanics, and chaos theory have contributed a great deal to creating these feelings.

person who wants proof, especially negative proof, and who will accept or deny claims based only on proof. In a way, that stance leaves the poor agnostic in a position in which he never fully believes anything, but he half-believes everything, because the possibilities are endless.

Someone came to visit Niels Bohr, one of the greatest physicists of the century. To his great astonishment, the visitor saw a horseshoe hanging on the doorway. After some time, when they had become friendly, he asked, "Professor Bohr, do you believe in horseshoes?" Bohr said, "Absolutely not." So the visitor asked, "Then why is one hanging in your doorway?" Bohr answered, "People say that it helps even if you do not believe in it."

We all know sane, intelligent people who will not go to synagogue or church because there is no proof for the existence of God, but who will talk about vibrations, or who use crystals to heal themselves, who avoid the unlucky number 13, or who consult an astrologer. To be sure, not all intelligent people in our era are prone to all of the New Age superstitions; some people prefer to adhere to slightly older ones, so they firmly believe in *New York Times* headlines, in the wisdom of the theater reviewer, or in psychoanalysis. The fountain of Faith is clearly gushing there.

This abundance of belief, however, does not include faith in God. Even opening oneself to the possibility of faith in God requires an effort. Modern societal norms are almost like a religion, compelling everybody to belong, to acquire, to look a certain way, to act a certain way. Society dictates, "Intelligent people don't do, or say, or believe in these things." Remember the expression, "It is un-American to do something like that"?* In order to extricate one-self from that compelling societal web, a person has to use a fair amount of disbelief, an ability to fight, to move against the stream. It takes learning and choice not to comply.

Although the ability to believe has not diminished, there is a deep mental gap between the things that people believe in, and faith in God. The distinction is not really rational; rather, it is one of perception. Those thousands of things that people normally accept with unquestioning trust are not perceived as requiring faith; they are considered "knowledge," or "common sense," while "faith" is required for things that are beyond the accepted norm of the time or society. Faith requires a jump, the proverbial leap of faith. There comes a point at which we have to jump to a conclusion that is not part of accepted knowledge.

This leap of faith is not easy. Faith, in the capital letter sense, is much harder than belief in everyday banalities, because it has so many mental and practical consequences. Many things are accepted without question because they are not considered important enough. For example, if I ask when Alexander the Great lived, people who remember history will give me the dates. Nobody doubts the existence of Alexander the Great. Why not?

*Or the older and more enduring "un-English," which would kill an idea or action in the heyday of the British Empire.

The actual proof is, in fact, quite scanty: some stories in books, and some antiquities that have been identified as belonging to the era of Alexander the Great. There is circumstantial evidence that may support a belief in the existence of Alexander the Great, but it is surely not as plain as the nose on my face.

Why is it, then, that people have no problem having faith in the existence of Alexander the Great? The reason is very simple: what do they care? If Alexander the Great did not exist, but rather was invented by somebody, so what? He is just one more figure in the world that is not entirely true. The existence or nonexistence of Alexander the Great has no real consequence in our lives. In the same way, we accept facts about the area of the Pacific Ocean, or about the wives of a sultan. These beliefs have no consequences, so it does not matter much whether we believe them or not.

Other beliefs are very demanding. Real Faith in important matters has consequences in one's life; it affects one's worldview and behavior, what one sees as right or wrong, one's values in life. This is not simple, unimportant knowledge that one can take or leave at will. If God exists, there are obviously vast implications. As long as people do not know what they believe, or are hazy about their beliefs (which is the way most people are), they can do whatever they want without thinking too much. People avoid thinking; it is easier that way.

Accepting a tenet of faith is not difficult; the hard part is accepting the attendant consequences. There are certain facts that we do not know from our own experience, but they are certainties. When a person becomes aware of them, that changes his life. Take, for example, mortality. We do not know about mortality from firsthand experience; we know about it from other people, but they do not count. We are alive, and we do not acknowledge our own mortality. When we become aware of this fact—whether at the age of two or at the age of sixty-two—then of course life is affected. Plans change, expectations change, priorities change. The belief that death exists is not, in itself, startling; accepting it, and coping with the implications, is always important and may sometimes be painful.

The second difficulty in making the leap of faith is that it is indeed a leap. One must be willing to decide to make the jump, and people do not make that leap unless they are compelled to do so. The compulsion is usually an inner drive triggered by questions that will not go away. Some people have philosophical-existential questions; Descartes' *Discourse on Method*[2] and Lewis Carroll's *Alice in Wonderland* use two different styles to deal with the same question, "What is real existence?" The prophet Isaiah (40:26) starts out from an entirely different point of departure, saying, "Lift up your eyes to Heaven and see who created these: He who brings out the starry host and calls each one by name."

However, these big questions—about existence, and about who created the universe and is responsible for the order of the world—are compelling for just a few. Most people, especially city dwellers, never see the stars. They have hardly any interest in lifting up their eyes, and when they do, what they see is lighted billboards. The questions which bring most people to Faith are, in the very simplest words, "What is the meaning of all this? What is the purpose?" These are questions that, basically, do not have answers—unless one makes the leap of faith. Each of us asks our own question in our own way, at our own time. Sometimes, questions are asked in a moment of crisis, but often, in the midst of ordinary life, a person will say to himself, "I have a busy life; I do things, I run from place to place, I live, I eat, I go through the motions, but where am I running to? What is the meaning and purpose of all this?" Then the search for an answer begins.

Walking through life is like wandering in a labyrinth, constantly probing and searching for the opening, the answer to that riddle. It is depressing enough when we feel that we are not getting anywhere, but the deepest despair is when one knows that the labyrinth has no way out, that one will wander aimlessly from corridor to corridor until death. We do not always think about meaning and purpose, but when this question does come to awareness, it becomes a haunting, gnawing pain. We want a response to our deep existential questions, and we want a nontrivial answer. We have trivial, temporary answers—too many of them. "I am here to make money" and "I am here to devour as many hamburgers as possible" may be purposes, but they are not fulfilling ones.

The very concept of purpose is essentially a religious statement, and the quest for purpose is a spiritual journey.

This may be an unpleasant revelation for some people, who vehemently claim that they are atheists or agnostics, that they do not believe in anything. Even people who see themselves as living in a labyrinth without an opening can nevertheless see life as a very dignified existence—an adventure filled with danger, challenge, and beauty, with opportunity to love, to pursue justice, to raise a family, and to care for others in the world. The grandeur and the challenge of that kind of existence do not seem trivial at all, even for people who believe that when they die, that is the end of it. That sense of the beauty, the grandeur, and the adventure give meaning and purpose to life. Without using God's name, that person is really a very believing person, with a deep faith that there is transcendental meaning in living the adventure of life in a dignified way.

That is the essence of faith. It is deep belief in things that cannot be proved. I cannot prove beauty, dignity, honesty, or integrity, yet I may live a life filled with all these things. A person who has nontrivial answers to these questions of purpose and meaning is, in one way or another, speaking about God—even if, for some inexplicable reason, he does not want to call it that. The atheist who is living a dignified, ethical, and spiritual life is an unconscious believer. If he were not fighting it so hard, he would realize that he has a formulation for his Faith, and if he put it in slightly different words, and arranged it slightly differently, it might almost be a well-organized religion. A rose, by any name, is still a rose; likewise God, by any name, is still God.

People may say that any question about purpose is an unscientific question.* That is indeed so. Science deals with only one part, one kind of pertinent human question; by its very definition, it does not, and cannot, address others. Scientific questions, mathematical questions, legal questions, and shoemaking questions each address different aspects of reality. The fact that our Faith questions cannot be answered with scientific, mathematical, legal, or shoemaking answers does not mean that they are irrelevant, unimportant, or not compelling. When someone falls in love, the question "Does he/she love me?" becomes a very important, all-consuming question, which one may ponder for hours, for days. It is not a scientific question, but it is a very important question for the people involved. In the same way, the question "What is the meaning of my running, my rushing, of all the small things and big things that I do?" is an important question.

Questions of Faith are not philosophical, sociological, or psychological; they are intensely personal. Everyone has to find his or her own way of dealing with them. The point at which a person is ready for a change, for a jump, is when that person becomes aware of the existence of the question. Once we become aware of the questions, this awareness pushes us toward the brink at which we have to

---

To be precise, this is true in regard to contemporary science; however, for many generations, scientists did deal with this problem, and some teleological trends appear every now and then in recent times as well.

leap. To put it in a parable, if you find yourself stranded in a place with ditches all around and no bridges, you must jump—or you will die in your little place. That jump becomes a necessity, not because people tell you or ask you to jump, but because there you are, in position. When one comes to that point, one can say, "I must make a choice: to jump or not to jump." Is it a matter of free will? Of course, we always have free choice. We do not always deserve great credit for what we do with our free will, but at some point, we do make choices.

This point of choice, the leap of faith, is made in a variety of ways. For some people, the moment of the leap to faith is an overwhelming, unforgettable experience; William James describes many such conversion experiences.[3] Many more people, however, never have an epiphany, but they still have faith. In the real life of both sinners and saints, faith is not always such a tremendous, overpowering emotional experience. Some people do not even know that they made the leap; they just take a step without even noticing, and then they find themselves on the other side. Only if they are introspective can they, perhaps, pinpoint the moment of change by retracing their personal history.

There are also quite a number of unconscious believers: very deep believers who just do not like the language, the way in which faith is commonly expressed. It is much easier for people in certain circumstances, or within a given social group, to give faith another name. They are not always Marranos (converts under coercion); nobody is forc-

ing them to believe one way or another, but they are unconscious of their faith. They live their lives without ever
knowing that they belong to the "flock of the believers,"
because they do not define themselves as such.

For some of these unconscious believers, the realization
"I have faith, I have always had faith, perhaps I have
never ceased believing since I was two years old" comes as
a shock. They are not accustomed to the idea, and therefore they feel that there is something wrong with them.
Nevertheless, although they may be going against the
grain of society, they are acknowledging a part of themselves that is a very natural aspect of existence.

In many cases, it is also a matter of probing. There
may be more believers outside the houses of prayer than
inside them. Some people with very deep Faith either do
not take to organized prayer, or do not agree with any particular theology, so they never participate in religious
groups or become members of an organized religion. With
all that, Faith is neither remote nor absolute. Rather, to
quote a Biblical passage: "It is not in Heaven. . . . Neither is it beyond the sea, but it is very near to you, in your
mouth and in your heart, that you may do it" (Deuteronomy 30:12–14).

Good Deeds

✢

M a n y highly moral people, including quite a few who
consider themselves deeply religious, have a certain notion about "little things." People say, or think, and—usually—act according to this idea: "Do you think that God
really cares about these little details? Do you think that
God cares about what I do in my kitchen, my bedroom, or
my office?"

What people consider insignificant depends on their
cultural and social environment, but it always reflects the
same seemingly broad-minded approach: big things matter; other, less important issues should not be taken seriously by intelligent people. These "unimportant" matters
are not necessarily things that people object to in principle; they may also be things that one is indifferent to, or

even considers beneficial, but nevertheless unimportant. These little things are a part of every religion. They may be positive deeds, such as attending prayer services or fulfilling religious commandments, or negative ones, like petty thefts or white lies. One may accept the lofty ideals and broad principles—but not the small details.

For some, this attitude may just be a cover for laziness; however, it also has a genuine religious, theological aspect. One is asking, Why should the Almighty care about my actions, whether good or bad? God is the ruler of the universe, where immense bodies, planets and stars, move as little dots within a myriad of spinning galaxies. Compared to these, what am I? Within a small framework— my family and friends—I may be important, but when I look at the world from a wider perspective of time and space, my activities and my very existence seem insignificant.

It seems, then, very strange to believe that the Master of all the world should bother about my little sin. Similarly, why should it be of any importance whether I give charity, or encourage a friend in need? This is equally true regarding prayer. When I ask for things, what are my chances of being heard at all? Is it not presumptuous, or worse, to believe that my praise, or my request, counts for anything at all?

This fundamental question bothers many people, either consciously or unconsciously. Some act as if there were no answer; others are annoyed and perplexed by it. In all cases, it stems from a certain kindergarten image of

God, which so many of us still retain: somebody with a long white beard, sitting somewhere in Heaven, thousands of miles above us, a stick in one hand and a package of candies in the other.

As adults, some of us replace that image—which we understand to be childish and inadequate—with the image of the boss. I think of an immediate, benign supervisor who cares about me; I come to him when I have complaints; he smiles when I give him a compliment, and if he is in a good mood, he may grant my request. If I do something wrong in the office, he may scold or even punish me. In big companies, there is somebody above the immediate supervisor; that person does not care so much about what I say, because he or she has very little direct contact with me. I am just a small unit in a big system. I would have to do something really horrible to be punished by the big boss, and it would have to be something entirely out of the ordinary for me to be remembered as the criminal who did it.

If I go further up the ladder, to an even bigger boss, the same pattern is amplified. Here, the small details do not really matter. The loss of a unit or a little skirmish may not even be reported to the commander of a big army. The President of the United States does not really know what people do in their offices, nor does he care. When citizens write him letters, some secretary answers them; only great, exceptional, famous individuals may sometimes merit a personal reply.

With all that, the President of the United States still

functions within a very limited sphere of power and influence, compared to the entire universe. If someone were responsible for our planet, or our solar system, or our galaxy, with its millions of stars and all their planets, as well as the galaxies beyond it, that person would obviously not deal with little details. If these do not matter, surely my actions are not even important enough to be registered. What chance does tiny me have of being heard, let alone answered?

People who picture the "Master of the Universe" as the "Biggest Boss" of all believe that they are expressing profound respect for God. They think that they are not like those picayune people who believe that God has nothing better to do than check the petty details of every individual's life. For even as a parent, how much do I know and care about every little thing that my children do? There are so many small details about which I am completely ignorant. I care about the big things. I may think that I have a broader view; I see the vastness of the universe, and therefore I infer that God cannot possibly have time for details.

But when I say that God does not deal with detail, I am in fact cutting God down to my own measure. No matter how much I enlarge it, it is still my own picture, extended: God is very important, a very important person, and therefore God is like the big boss, a big ruler, a big president—only more so. However big I may make it, it still remains basically an enlargement of a small human picture.

The reason a human boss does not know or care about what happens to the paper clips in the office is that he has a limited mind. Only certain things can fit into a limited storage house; the rest has to be discarded. The boss must therefore decide what is important to him and what is not; he cannot afford to clutter his mind with minute, irrelevant details, or his functioning will be hampered. The bigger the boss, the greater the number of details, and therefore the more generalized the items with which he can deal. If we say that God does not care about this or that, it actually means that we cast God in the big boss image.

Unlike the biggest of bosses, though, God is infinite. Infinity is a difficult concept, even in mathematics. In relation to God, it is more difficult yet. Something infinite has no boundaries; there is no limit to the number of details it can contain. Moreover, it is a basic mathematical fact that compared to infinity, every other number is zero, and every other size is equal. One million, or two thousand quadrillion, when compared to infinity, are both exactly zero. Theologically, saying that God is infinite means that all the details become equally insignificant, regardless of their size. In that sense, a galaxy, with all the gigantic stars it contains, is exactly equal to the smallest particles of an atom.

Therefore, if it makes any sense for God to care about what happens to a galaxy, it makes exactly the same amount of sense for God to care about what happens to a blade of grass. Compared to God, they are of exactly the same magnitude. If God cares for the whole universe (which, however big it may be, is still limited), then all its little parts are of equal importance in God's eyes. If one thousand people, a hundred thousand people, or five billion people cry out in prayer, or if one little child prays, they are heard equally; the number does not make any difference. When the stars sing, or a little bird sings, they are all heard equally.

In one of the Jewish prayers we say that God "is immutable, and treats small and great alike."[1] This is one way of expressing the idea that the differences between big and small, important and unimportant, beautiful and ugly, are insignificant to the One who is Infinite, who is beyond all limitations, the One for whom limitations are meaningless. Similarly, Psalm 139 says, "If I ascend to Heaven, there You are; if I go down to Hell, I find You."* To God, says this psalm, Heaven and earth, the very far and the very close, darkness and light, are all the same.

To use a high-tech analogy, computers can make calculations with very large numbers. There is no computer that can deal with infinite numbers, since even the strongest computer is, after all, quite limited. However, for the sake of illustration, suppose there were such a computer; would it be able to do complex mathematical operations with immense sums, but not be able to add two

*Rabbi Avraham Ibn Ezra (1089—1164), one of the greatest poets and philosophers of the Middle Ages, wrote that this psalm is the most important one in the Book of Psalms.

and two? If we say that a computer can deal only with big principles, but not with small details, then in fact we are saying that it does not work at all.

Chapter 113 in the Book of Psalms (especially verses 4–5) expresses a similar idea. On the one hand, the chapter says, "The Lord is high above all nations; His glory transcends the Heavens." The feeling that God is distant, above and beyond everything, seems to be part of God's glory. Yet the Psalm continues, "Who is like the Lord our God who dwells on high [yet] looks down so low upon heaven and earth." Some people want to praise God by saying that He is so vast that His glory is in Heaven. However, by saying that, they are also implying that it is *only* there, and therefore I am entitled to do anything I wish, be it in the privacy of my home or in my business. If God is so great, I can easily smuggle the little things behind God's back. This great God may not listen to me, but also will not scold me, so I am safe.

However, this psalm goes on to say that God is much greater than this. God looks down on Heaven, and if so, then God also looks down on earth. The Infinite is really everywhere, and therefore Heaven and earth are exactly the same. In God's eyes, an archangel is no more important than a mouse. Being the small and limited creatures that we are, there is, for us, a tremendous difference between the molehill and the mountain. For God, this difference is insignificant.

In other words, the capacity to look at details is part of Infinity—in fact, it is one of the definitions of being infinite. Just as nothing is too big for God, so, too, nothing is too small for God. Nothing is insignificant or small enough to go unnoticed, because God has an all-encompassing view that contains absolutely everything. Therefore, the belief that something is so insignificant that it can escape God's attention is worse than blasphemy: it is nonsense. The very notion of facing the Infinite means facing it down to the last detail, and the tiniest detail becomes as significant as one's whole being.

But does God care at all? Why should God care? For me, as a human being, my life, my business, or my goldfish may be very important; but I am limited in every sense, and therefore many things bother or gladden me. God is infinite; why should the Almighty care for the whole universe, as huge as it may seem to me?

It is very difficult to give an answer on God's behalf; but we can say that He obviously does care. For some inexplicable reason, God bothered to create the world, and form quite elaborate rules (which we call "laws of nature") for its functioning—and that means that God cares. The world may be, for God, a plaything or an experiment—but He bothered to have it. Since the world exists, one cannot say that God is so vast as not to be aware of it, and in some way, care for it.

Therefore, if I do something wrong, my little wrongdoing is as important as my whole lifetime, and my barely expressed thought is as significant as the most glorious epic poem. The cry of a little child weeping in bed is as audible to God as what the President of the United States says in a public address transmitted from coast to coast. It is only the idolatry of making God in a finite size, with finite knowledge, that gives rise to the question, "Does God care?" with all its ensuing confusion.

Having a more mature, far more abstract notion of God results not in making God more remote; rather, it makes God much closer to us. However, it does not bring along an easy sentimental answer for so many other problems that face us in our relationship with the Almighty. There is, and always will be, a discrepancy, a gap, between our very human desires and dreams, and reality. The true answers to questions may not be those that we would like to hear. Even so, a better understanding saves a great deal of the emotional anguish that results from having wrong expectations.

Thus, even when we accept the premise that God hears everything, including our prayers, another question arises: is it reasonable to expect a response?* Somehow, people have the idea that their prayers deserve a response that will be the fulfillment of that prayer. In our world, however, everyone knows that a petition may be received and read, and the answer may still be "No." So, too, it may happen with prayer; there is a possibility that the answer to a prayer—even if prayed fervently and with all

*The Zen method is to ponder, query, and ask questions—some of which may be pure, while others are quite nasty—until, possibly, one achieves a tranquillity in which asking and answering are no longer necessary. Prayer is a different process.

goodwill and sincere intentions—will just be "No." Often people have an expectation that whenever they ask for something—or at least when they ask God for it—they must get it. This may be called "the spoiled brat philosophy." In prayer, too, one pleads for an answer, or for an explanation, but the response may not satisfy the request.

Only very occasionally does one get a direct, explicit answer.* Sometimes a partial answer comes to us many years later. Something I once did, which at the time seemed pointless or wrong, in retrospect may turn out to have been a very important and successful action. I may expect lightning to strike me whenever I do something wrong, but the lightning may come in God's good time, which is, most probably, when I least expect it. Many times, the answer— which is the most appropriate one—is silence. And we may very well go through life—at least life in this world—without getting any answer whatsoever.

The desire for explanations is a very understandable human need. We want to hear the truth, and we want to understand why and for what purpose a certain thing happened. However, we also have another, simultaneous wish: we expect this truth to be easily understood. These two wishes are, in most cases, mutually exclusive. Our assumptions about our ability to understand are often quite

*See, for example, the end of the Book of Job. As for those people who are positive that they do get such answers, only in a minority of the cases is this true; mostly, this is the product of imagination, illusion, or even neurosis.

presumptuous. Often, when we do get an explanation, we are unable to understand it. Our thinking process is not only heavily biased by our wishes and inclinations, but is inherently limited. A full reply may be unpleasant to hear, and generally, far above our ability to comprehend.

That does not mean, however, that we ought not to question. The prophet Jeremiah (12:1) says, "You are righteous, O Lord, and I cannot disagree with You, yet let me talk with You of Your judgments." In other words, God is, by definition, right, but we are entitled to disagree, and even to express our disagreement. If we are hurt, and suffer, we have a perfect right to cry out. Indeed, if we pretend that it does not hurt, then we are liars.[2] In fact, the oldest ritual of Jewish national life, which is a few thousand years old, is the Seder night—the first night of the Passover festival. That ritual begins today, as it did long ago, with children asking questions. If they cannot ask on their own, somebody is supposed to teach them how to ask questions. We are instructed to start out with questions. Asking questions is not only permissible, it is encouraged. When one has a bothersome question, one should ask it.

Moreover, in the face of any evil, we not only have the need, but also the right, and even the duty, to ask, and to demand answers. Yet no one promises us that we will get an answer—or that, if we do, we will be able to understand it.

The questions posed by the Holocaust are not different, in principle, from those raised by the heartbreaking experience of visiting a children's cancer ward. Whether it is Jews, children, or little mice, the question is basically the same: does each and every living being matter to God?

Many times the Bible describes the concept of redemption as a birth. Redemption will also come with pain, blood, and a fair amount of screaming. We are allowed to scream; we are allowed to say, "You may be right, but I want to know why!" Someday we will all pass on to another, clearer world and have a different view of the Almighty. Then we will either be able to complain properly, or we will no longer have any need to complain.

In the realm of theology, the philosopher and the believer ask basically the same question, but from two very different angles, which are like a circle and its center. The philosopher says, "The world exists, so how can there be a God?" He is trying to find a way from the circumference to the center. The believer, on the other hand, says, "God exists; how, then, can there be a world?" He tries to find a path connecting the center to the circumference. Sometimes, both the philosopher and the believer are successful; they find good answers, and they meet. When they fail, however, each of them is left with the question. If one could choose, I think that rather than being left with the question "I am in the world; how can God exist?" it is far better to be left with "I am with God, I just do not understand how this world can exist."

Sex

So much has been said about sex. Sex is exhilarating, the highest expression of love; or, to some people, it is dirty and shameful. In any case, it has always fascinated human beings. It is a universal human experience, and a very complex one, which takes a great deal of our time and energy, and it is always connected with very strong emotions, both positive and negative.

In this chapter, I am not going to be discussing love, family, or morals, nor am I going to be judgmental as to what is or is not perverse. My intention here is to try to understand some of our fascination with sex, as well as some of the fundamental problems connected with it. What is it about sex that makes it so enticing?

A factual description of what sex is—meaning, the

purely physical act and response—is rather simple, and may be quite uninteresting as a subject. Such a description would be something like "the mutual rubbing of two erogenous zones." This, however, does not explain the interest, the fascination, the fact that people deal with sex so much—thinking, dreaming, and talking about it beforehand, getting involved in the act itself, and remembering it later on—for all this is not entirely based on the mere physical response. The physical response is a part of it, but only a part, and it can neither explain nor justify our intense involvement.

Sex is not a unique human phenomenon; it is almost universal among living beings: nice ones and ugly ones, bees and spiders, gazelles and monkeys, vegetables and flowers. Even in microbes, which in most cases regenerate by simply splitting themselves in two, we can see, from time to time, something akin to a sexual act, when two cells combine, reshuffle, and change themselves.

In the biological world, sex appears in a great variety of forms, which can be very informative and help us not only to know how other creatures have sex, but also to understand ourselves: in what ways are we human? How are we similar to other creatures? What are the things that set us apart from the rest of the world? This knowledge has great significance for us. The speedily changing notions of acceptable behavior and mores only enhance our need to know what is essential and permanent.

In most of the biological world, sex is a process that is just the means for procreation, the continuation of the species. Although there are exceptions even within the biological world, that is the general rule. Yet, in all its many forms, sex is one of the most powerful, most compelling drives within all creatures. In fact, in some creatures, the compulsion to engage in sexual activity may be stronger than all the other basic drives in life, even hunger or self-preservation. For the males of many species, indulging in sex is dangerous, not from the moral point of view, but physically. Some species take months to migrate to their breeding areas, or compete so strenuously that many of them die in the attempt to mate. The delicate female praying mantis actually chops off the male's head during their sexual intercourse, and eats the rest of him afterward.

Moreover, the universal sexual compulsion does not necessarily have much to do with feelings of pleasure or enjoyment in erogenous zones. In most fish, for example, the male and female have elaborate courtship rituals, and strange reproductive habits, but they do not even touch, and their fertilization happens outside their bodies. Their enjoyment, to the extent that it exists, possibly comes from fulfilling the compulsion, and not from what seems to be the central aspect of sex to us humans—the tactile pleasures. For most creatures, sex exists only as a means to an end. There is an unbreakable connection between the sexual act and its biological purpose—procreation. Most female mammals (and some males) have a period of "heat" during which they are fertile, and ready for sexual response; sex occurs at no other time.

Here, we humans differ from the rest of zoology. For us, sex is not necessarily bound to procreation. In fact, these are two independent areas; the connection between them has been severed, and we can have the pleasure without ever fulfilling the biological purpose.*

As a result of cutting the tie between the sexual act and its biological, reproductive goal, we humans are left with a very strong, very compelling desire that does not have a specific biological purpose. This is the reason why we are afraid of sex—or at least we are wary of it. There is a universal human reaction toward sex, which is unlike our emotional responses to other physical needs and desires. This is expressed in a variety of forms: in elaborate public rituals, or in a feeling of fear and embarrassment. Coyness and play, as well as secrecy and denial, all arise from the feeling that we have a devil within us, a random, wild desire with no intrinsic, natural limits.

We know of thousands of human societies, in the past and in the present, each very different from the other. Societies differ in the ways in which they understand the world and themselves, in what they judge as desirable or repulsive, or as important or unimportant, in the roles that society members are assigned, and in the variety of ways that people relate to each other. Thus there are, for example, societies that impose various limitations on eating, and others

---

In some primitive societies, people did not even know that there was a connection. Sex was done for its own sake, while pregnancies were attributed to unearthly beings.

that have hardly any inhibitions or prohibitions about food. This derives from the fact that eating has natural limits; it is done to satisfy a well-defined physiological need for nutrition, and there is a limit to the amount of food we are capable of eating. This is also the case with sleeping and with movement, which are defined and self-limited.

However, every society in the world has some taboos about sexual matters. They are not the same everywhere; some prohibitions seem to be far more common, some are specific to a single culture, but there are always some taboos. These prohibitions, these self-imposed limitations, are not biological. People can have sex with anybody—one might almost say with anything—and there is no biological barrier. In humans, sexual desire can arise between partners who are incapable of reproducing, and can be expressed in ways in which procreation is physiologically impossible. Some contraceptive means have been known since antiquity, and they serve as a further separation between sex and procreation. In our modern, technologically advanced culture, the birth control pill has effectively made this separation both easy and widespread. This happened faster than changes in the general culture, with unforeseen consequences.

Animals do not have sexual taboos or rules of sexual behavior because they do not need them; in animals, sex is limited by natural forces. The desire and the purpose are tied together, and the desire will only spring forth in the right context, when it makes biological sense. For us, sexual desire has no intrinsic limitations, and therefore we feel that it has to be kept within bounds in some other way. We impose moral, societal, religious limits—all of which are meant to confine this desire to certain times, places, and contexts.

In our times, as boundaries are becoming hazier, less stringent, and less powerful, many forms of sexual behavior are proliferating. Whether you call them deviations or alternatives, they all clearly demonstrate that the connection between the biological purpose and the practice of sex is becoming looser over time. As these inhibitions, prohibitions, or limits have weakened, sexual desire has gained complete independence. In some places, it has even become the ruler of the society. Physical sexuality—pleasure without purpose—gets a lot of advertisement, and it is glorified in our popular culture.

We humans are astute beings capable of making abstractions, even if they do not always make sense. We can conceive of matter that exists without form, and form without matter, but the fact that we can imagine them does not mean that they can actually exist. Because the sexual act can be done as a physiological exercise with anybody, in any form, without any emotional content, we think we are capable of separating sexual activity from emotion, both conceptually and in practice. We think we can have sex without emotion, and emotion without sex.

However, this complete separation exists only in theory. In reality, emotional relationships, physiological compulsion, and sexual activity (or even sexual fantasy) interconnect and create a whole that is greater than the sum of its parts. When we cut them asunder, each aspect becomes a one-dimensional monster. Without context and meaning, the sexual act becomes reduced to a simple physiological process, limited and uninteresting. In the beginning of this century, the very modern people said that having sex is just like drinking a glass of water.[1] Eventually, it does indeed become just as interesting as drinking a glass of water. Although it is physiologically possible for our sexual appetite to wander, doing biologically purposeless acts, it does not make sense for the whole human being, who contains a multitude of layers, both emotional and cognitive.

When sexuality goes beyond the limitations and the framework of emotional significance, it self-destructs, not in a moral sense, but in a pragmatic one. When people circumscribe the pleasure of sex, separate it from a meaningful relationship, and make that limited pleasure the sole aim, the more they succeed, the less pleasurable sex becomes. The less emotional contact there is, the less fascinating and the less meaningful sex is. The physiological response still occurs, but the fascination dissipates, and soon the enjoyment; in fact, it sometimes becomes downright unappealing. The independent, purely bodily sex is, in this sense, like a small Third World state: a very poor place indeed.

Sexuality is complicated, and composed of many interconnected parts. All these essential components are apparent in the conscious mind, in various degrees. Culture and environment push some of them forward, making people more aware of their presence, while others are felt only dimly, or are completely hidden within the uncon-

scious. Some of the most powerful primeval forces are so
deeply submerged that one may describe them as belonging to the archetypal, collective unconscious.

The most primal and powerful part is the compulsion
to fulfill the biological imperative to reproduce—the same
compulsion that we see in every species, from the lowest
to the highest, that makes the flowers bloom and the
fungi shed their spores. Courtship, the ritualized prelude
to sex, is another universal, not exclusively human, behavior; it is a biologically programmed behavior, built
into the sexual drive.

After these most primitive and general drives comes
the other, higher level,* which demands a partnership,
and creates a sense of closeness and trust. The idea of
having not just any partner, but a partner with whom one
has an emotional relationship, is not just a romantic, cul-
turally determined concept. The love element in the sexual relationship is an essential part of the connection.
Speaking about love between animals or birds may be incorrect, anthropomorphic language;[2] however, animals do
behave in ways that we consider expressions of love when
done by humans.

The urge to create and maintain closeness and partnership does not come only from one's cultural upbringing. It
is a part of the most basic urge, which dwells in the most
primitive part of the brain, possibly within the DNA in the

*Higher, in the sense that it is found in more advanced crea-
tures.*

living cells. This desire to connect is inherent within the sexual drive itself. The other ramifications—the pleasure, the enjoyment, and the play—are additional ways to entice or strengthen the primary levels of connection. When we try to enhance the secondary aspects and kill the primary driving force, we cannot succeed. We can maintain it for a time, but it runs counter to the forces of evolution.

In humans, the physical pleasure is an incentive to engage in sexual activity, but essentially, it is not necessary, as we saw from the animals that reproduce without touching. Physical pleasure has no intrinsic reproductive purpose, but it does have a role in creating intimacy and love, and these create the context for the sexual activity. In humans, that loving intimacy is necessary in order to give sex meaning, so that it is not a flat picture, but a multidimensional one.

Although we can separate sex from emotion, when we do so, neither aspect of the sexual connection, by itself, can be fully alive. When we dissect ourselves into parts, sex becomes a physiological, nerve-ends pleasure, independent of any other considerations. That dissociation kills the internal integrity and meaning of sexuality. This is not a moral or theological issue at all; it is a biological fact. It has nothing to do with family, or monogamy, or values. Humans form couples, families, communities, and societies, but love, family, and fidelity are not necessary corollaries of sex. It is our human nature, our cultural traditions, and our religious sensibilities that dictate how we work out these relationships.

Some commentators say that Eve and Adam's sin was in

cutting the natural bond between sex and breeding.[3] As we said, this cutting apart turns the sexual drive into something strange, something wrong, and as a result, many cultures connect sex with sin (which, by the way, does not always diminish the pleasure; in many cases, it makes it more intriguing and enjoyable—if only temporarily).[4] In fact, when the deeper levels of sex disappear as a result of certain cultural phenomena, and only the physical act prevails, it becomes unsatisfying. Therefore, there is a need to "spice" sex. Sin and perversion (in any form that these are conceived in any specific society) may alleviate the blandness of the act itself—for a while. However, in the long run, even these cannot replace the lack of the deeper, more essential elements. One-dimensional sex becomes, again, what it is: a physical exercise, with a very limited reward.

Adam and Casanova represent two extremes. Adam is the man with one wife, one and only one, who is for him a mate, a friend, "flesh of his flesh" (Genesis 2:23), and the mother of all children. Casanova has no wife, but does have any number of women; he is searching for variety, for the different or the bizarre, enjoying the sexual act as a purpose in itself. Both these extremes exist within each of us, and we strive to find a median between them; we seek some combination of these two in our own behavior, and in our relationships. It is not easy, it is not simple, and it is never the same for two people—because they have different responses, because they are separate individuals. Working out the conflicting parts within us and between us, and weaving them into a meaningful tapestry, is hard work. The connection between two human beings is not without friction and stress, even in Paradise, as we see from the description of Adam and Eve's problems in the first chapters of Genesis.

Jewish tradition, however, does not see sex, per se, as sinful. In fact, in the right context, and when engaged in with conscious purpose, sex is seen as a positive commandment, a force of connection—because, in contrast to food and money, sexual pleasure in itself is not connected with ownership. It is a pleasure that is derived from giving and being connected with another—both in the body and beyond the physical plane; it can become a most meaningful expression of love, of charity and benevolence. Sexual desire, possibly the most powerful human desire, can become an expression of holiness.

The physical union enhances the spiritual union of two individuals. More than that, the particular bond between male and female, in which giving and receiving blend with each other, becomes a way of learning and experiencing a multilevel connection. In a nonabstract form, it becomes a paradigm for doing good deeds. Study and prayer, as well as charity, may also acquire some kind of erotic fervor. This is the reason why Kabbalistic literature describes any kind of deep connection between spiritual entities with the term "copulation."

Strangely enough, it seems that we can learn from the birds and the beasts of the field that we are not just expressions of our physiology, that our sexuality can have aim and purpose, that we are capable of love, sharing, connection, and holiness. Perhaps, then, looking back into the animal kingdom can help us become fully human again.

Death

❧

Death is frightening.

The quality and quantity of this fear may vary, depending on age, personality, and direct encounters with death, but to most people, death is frightening.

There are three reasons why people are afraid of death. First, it is an irreversible process. There is something very frightening about the idea of going somewhere and not being able to return. Second, it is totally unknown. Anything completely unknown is scary.

Neither of these reasons, however, really explains our fear of death. Life is full of irreversible events. We age, and although some people try to reverse time and look twenty years younger than they are, time is not reversible. Within any normal life span, many irreversible changes

happen. In fact, life itself is an irreversible event. Moreover, death is a part of the normal process of being, and as
such, we should relate to it as just one more event in a
continuous process.

In addition, many other unknown things are not as
frightening. Indeed, they generate a range of feelings:
uneasiness, suspense, curiosity, sometimes eager anticipa-
tion, and even hope. Death, however, is not usually connected with hope (except, perhaps, for people who commit
suicide), nor is it connected with genuine curiosity or ea-
gerness.

The third and possibly most frightening aspect of
death is the notion of annihilation. Death is not just a
change—experiencing a new event or entering a new
phase—but rather, a total cessation of being; one ceases to
exist as a person. Everything stops. Everything disap-
pears. The annihilation of death is something we can
hardly imagine, and it is extremely hard to accept. Existence means "I am here. I am alive. I know what is hap-
pening to me." We are unable to grasp that it will all stop,
that our existence—which for each of us is the center of
the universe—will not continue.

Of course, this notion of total cessation is connected
with only one part of our existence—the bodily part. We
can all see what happens to the body after death. However, our existence does not stop completely with death;
another part of our being, the nonbodily part, remains. In
death, as in life, we are compound beings made of two un-
equal, disparate parts. One part is visible and has a par-

ticular way of being and communicating; the other, inner part is in many ways—though not entirely—what we call the "self." During one's lifetime, that self is a combination of body and soul, which does not dwell entirely in the soul, nor entirely in the body. The interface between body and soul creates our sense of self.

Death is an abrupt and very dramatic change, in which this point of self—which during life shifts and changes between body and soul, combining and connecting them in a unique bond—stops its interplay. The self moves into a very different, completely nonmaterial existence. This shift causes the terror of death, because we cannot cope with such a dramatic change.

There is an image, found on a tablet from the Minoan culture in Crete of some four thousand years ago. On one side of the tablet is a drawing of a person walking, then of a person lying down, apparently dead, and a small bird-like figurine, which probably represents the soul. On the other side are a caterpillar, a chrysalis, and a butterfly.

There is no way to determine the tablet's original intent; to my mind, however, it seems to be depicting precisely that dramatic change. For the caterpillar, changing into a butterfly is exactly the same as dying is for humans. In other words, the caterpillar cannot imagine life as a butterfly. When the caterpillar goes into the chrysalis, it dies; in a sense, it ceases to exist as a caterpillar. When it reemerges, it is the same caterpillar that reemerges— and yet it is not the same. It is entirely different; it has an entirely different life, an entirely different existence. Nei-

ther of the two stages is understood by the other. Not only
is the caterpillar unable to imagine life as a butterfly, the
butterfly does not know its life as a caterpillar at all, even
though the caterpillar has begotten it.

That image—whether the Minoan stone intended it as
such, or it is just my interpretation—is a rudimentary
portrayal of what happens at death. When we die, everything pertaining to our former existence ceases. We
reemerge in an entirely different form, one that is not understandable in life. Though we have a soul when we are
alive, our soul is only part of our existence—and not always the most conscious part of the self. It may be a living
and thinking part, but the soul alone does not have the
same self-understanding as it has when it is together with
the body. Because of the way we are raised, because of the
way we live, we do not have the same feelings for the soul
as we have for the body.

In our times, it seems that people are more afraid to
confront death than ever before. Although death is depicted frequently on television and in movies, people really do not want to deal with it. Life has become, in many
senses, far more physical. Since the change into a non-
physical existence is frightening just to think about, we
try to block it from our awareness in whatever way we
can. This is also one of the reasons for the revival of the
very ancient practice of embalming the dead. In some
modern cemeteries, one almost expects to see the furniture, pets, perhaps also a spouse, sent to the grave to ac-
company the dead. Even though the belief in the efficacy

of these things has lessened on the way from ancient Egypt or Sumer, the desire to cling to the material has not diminished.

While in the caterpillar stage, so to speak, any inkling we have of an existence after death can only be based on images, metaphors, symbols, and pictures that are fundamentally untrue. Since we see the world through the lens of our bodily existence, we describe both life and death through physical, bodily images. These images, though they are never right or true, enable us to grapple with a completely different existence. Most of the symbolism, in any culture, cannot be taken literally. If one believes, say, that after death one will have wings, they will not be wings in the same sense as in this world.

The imagery of life after death does not depict reality in any way; it can only be understood allegorically, as symbolizing a different state of existence. We are unable to describe something that is so completely different—we just do not have the right words. People who survive clinical death are unable to report exactly what happened, because they have to use images from life here in this world for something that is otherworldly. Whatever they say is in some way nonsensical; there is an unbridgeable gap between the near-death experience and life. The images we have help us create an emotional relationship to death, but they are no more than our body-bound emotional reactions.

Even though we cannot really bridge the gap between life in the body and life without a body, we may at least get some ideas about what happens on the other bank. In doing so, we have to try to ignore, as much as possible, the figurative imagery, and get to more abstract notions. These may be only extrapolations of our experiences in the body, but still, they may be closer to the truth.

Although our experiences in the body are mainly through the bodily senses, we do have, in everyday life, a fair number of nonsensory experiences.* These are forms of perception that belong more to the soul than the body, albeit carried by the material brain. Two common ones are memory and imagination. Most people can remember past experiences very vividly (mostly visual images, but also sounds, and for some even smells and tactile experiences). Not only can we remember, we can also construct images that we have never actually encountered. The powers of memory and imagination differ among individuals, but for a fair percentage of people, these are strong enough to arouse physical responses, no less than those created by direct sensory experience.

Dreams are just as common. In our dreams, we do and watch things which, while we are dreaming, feel as real as life itself. There are many psychological theories—from Freud to behaviorism—that try to explain what triggers dreams, but even when we assume that the trigger is purely physical, the story of the dream is surely nonphys-

These experiences are not identical with extrasensory perception (ESP). That is a subject in itself, in which one needs to sift a lot of lies and fabrications from the truth, and which is also not universal.

ical. Therefore, all of us have many experiences of a non-physical life of some sort, which may give us a better understanding of a completely nonbodily existence.

Let us look at a few aspects of the Jewish view of death. At the moment of death—whether the parting is painful, or a moment of great joy, release, and freedom[1]—the soul carries all the imagery of life in the body with it to another existence.* All the soul's images and ways of thinking are bound up with life in a body, especially after a long life of seventy or eighty years. Although in death these "embodied" notions are no longer true, there is a certain period, which may be short or long, in which the soul behaves as if it were still within a body. In Hebrew, this imaginary world is called *'Olam ha-Dimyon*[2]—"the world of imagination."

All our experiences in life are internal. Philosophically speaking, there is no real proof of the existence of an external world. Therefore, after death, a person can continue to exist as a soul in *'Olam ha-Dimyon,* in an imaginary world in which everything continues as usual. The soul goes back to work, it meets friends, it leads a whole sham existence which is a continuation of the busy life that it had before: meetings, briefings, troubles with a spouse, problems with children, a machine that broke down, and so on—all in a

"Another existence" has meaning only in a nonphysical sense. We cannot speak about the next world as being next door, as being somewhere in the stratosphere or below the crust of the earth.

nonphysical existence built entirely of bodily images, none of which is real anymore.

A metaphor for this very strong experience of a reality that is subjective, imaginary, and completely untrue is the phenomenon of "phantom pain." When a part of the body is amputated, the person can often feel an itch or a pain in the limb that no longer exists. This happens because the body retains the image of the limb, sometimes for a while, sometimes forever. Although the person knows, and can even see with his eyes that the limb is no longer there, internally the person cannot make the transformation necessary to accept the new idea that this part does not exist. Such a transformation is even more difficult when the connection is far closer, deeper, and more thoroughgoing—namely, the connection to the whole body, to bodily existence.

After death, the soul carries with it a phantom image of its own existence. A soul that is not prepared for death, for moving on to another existence, may carry this phantom imagery for a long time before it can be released. There are many stories about people who are caught in such a world;[3] sometimes, the soul knows that it is dead, but cannot extricate itself from the grip of the internal universe it has brought with it from life. It may also happen that a person is not aware of his death. This is a sometimes ridiculous, sometimes frightening virtual reality. Thus, a person whose image of supreme joy in life was driving a carriage with four horses on a smooth road will be driving those horses on and on, on the smooth, endless road of *'Olam ha-Dimyon.*

The next stage in the journey of the soul is called, in Hebrew, *Kaf ha-Kela'*—literally, "the cup of a slingshot."[4] Again, to use physical images, this is the experience of being tossed about from one end of the universe to the other. One way of understanding *Kaf ha-Kela'* is that during this phase one sees the reality of one's life. Without the boundaries of the physical brain, which can block many things, the soul has complete recall of the events of its life, with an understanding possible only from the vantage point of a different form of existence. In life, we can remember only what happened in the past. *Kaf ha-Kela'* is reexperiencing life as it was, but with the additional perspective of knowing what will happen later, being able to see both ways.[5]

Being in *Kaf ha-Kela'* is like seeing life as an endless film loop, telling and retelling the same story. With each repetition, some things are blurred while others are highlighted, refining and deepening the soul's understanding of what it had and what it lacked, of what was important and what was unimportant, of what was right and what was wrong. The soul now has a completely different view, and has to measure itself against different criteria. Though it may have known about these standards during its earthly lifetime, they probably seemed very unreal then. For many people, doing a good deed or a terribly bad deed is far less important than eating a good meal or having indigestion. When we are disembodied, and view life as a whole, many things that we considered extremely important at the time turn out to be ridiculous and unessential, devoid of real meaning.

This may be somewhat similar to the way adults view their childhood. As adults, we remember our child-self with an adult understanding and a different perspective. Things that preoccupied us in childhood become either funny little anecdotes, ridiculous and immaterial, or embarrassing and shameful incidents. In *Kaf ha-Kela'* we see our every mistake, every blunder, every stupidity; we realize how much time, effort, enthusiasm, and life were put into things that ultimately have no real value. The more we see, the more penetrating the understanding, and the deeper the regret. We see life with full understanding of its meaning, but we are utterly unable to do anything about it. The soul then tries to do the impossible—to change events that cannot be changed, or at least, by looking at them again, to rectify them in some way.

In a way, old age, when the body becomes less dominant, is, for many of us, a preparation for the dissociation of body and soul. Therefore, for some people, old age may be a time of great tranquillity and serenity, as the body and its wishes and desires become weaker, and the soul can shine undisturbed. For others, whose conscious mind was always, and wholly, defined by their body, it is a period full of anguish, since their desires remain with them, although they can no longer be satisfied. Teleologically speaking, however, old age eases the final blow of death.

Similarly, this stage of *Kaf ha-Kela'* is a preparation for the next stage. This process, which is in many ways a painful one, is the reeducation of the soul. There is no repair for the soul, unless it is based on understanding. To be healed, one must learn that one is sick. To complete and rebuild, one has to conceive clearly what is lacking, what needs repair.

Reviewing one's whole life in this way is terrifying, but it is part of the process of release, of dissociating the two partners, and of coming into a different existence. Seeing life from outside the body grants us the ability to see the body—with which we were formerly so identified, and which we considered to be the senior partner in the body-soul relationship—as a slightly ridiculous naked ape, as four-dimensional protein moving through space.

Once we are out of the body, we also begin to understand how enslaved we were to the body that belonged to us. Imagine owning a car and having your whole life bound up with it, your entire daily schedule revolving around it: washing it, putting gasoline into it, driving it, parking it. It is as if the car is the whole of life, and you are just a driver. When this tremendous change in imagery occurs, the soul realizes that it is no longer subject to its vehicle, and it can then continue its life, moving on to an entirely different realm, disconnected from the body.

The stage after this release is called *Gehinnom*,[6] Hell. It is a continuation of this first preparatory stage of understanding. There are many images of Hell in various world cultures. Jews have devoted relatively little time to the concept, but they do have some Hell images of their own. In Jewish thought, Hell is not a punishment, but rather—to use a modern idiom—like going into deep therapy. Once we gain a better understanding of our existence from the completely different perspective of the pure soul,

once we realize how terrible some of our life experiences
were, those memories that still stick to us from the past
become too painful, and we want to get rid of them.

This second parting, dismissing one's former faults, is
what we call the pains of Hell. Life's transgressions are
not just a matter of having violated a law written in a
book; the deeds make an imprint on the soul. Seeing one's
mistakes in this way can be compared to waking up one
day and seeing all kinds of terrible things growing out of
one's body: thorns and horns, and other horrible growths.
One would desperately want to get rid of them, to cut
them off, but this is not plastic surgery; the cutting off is
accomplished only through the pain of understanding.
That, in itself, is Hell. The deeper the transgression, the
more deeply it is ingrained within the soul; the greater
the attachment to the world, the stronger the impact on
the soul, and, therefore, the greater the pain of cleansing,
and the deeper the level of Hell.

This process goes on in a way we cannot really measure
using earthly units of time. In Jewish thought there is no
everlasting Hell.[7] The time needed to purify each soul,
and to turn into an entirely different being, depends
largely on the person's life.[8] For those who have relatively
little to be ashamed of in their lives, it is short and easy;
their souls did not have too many ugly blemishes and dis-
tortions. For others who did not have the time and the
ability to regret and to change in their lifetime, the
process takes longer, like that of straightening somebody
who is completely crooked. Only then, once a person has

been cleansed, so to speak, can the next stage come, which we call Paradise.

As is the case with Hell, Paradise is not discussed very much in Jewish thought, since Judaism deals mainly with the here and now. Here, too, metaphorical imagery does not make any sense when we are addressing matters that our conscious mind, tied to our physical senses and perception, cannot grasp. One who is born blind cannot understand what color is; one who is bound by matter cannot understand a spiritual existence.[9] Whether the images that one has are images of wings and harps, or of being surrounded by beautiful orchards and fascinating meadows, these are not just impossible for a soul, they are misleading to the literal-minded. What Jewish tradition speaks of is a different "world," in which the soul enjoys the light of the Divine Presence. Those who have experienced a moment of bliss, the supreme joy of encountering new knowledge, or the delight of a moment of deep spirituality, at least have a hint of it.

The body has a rather low threshold not only for pain, but also for enjoyment; our bodily receptors make it impossible for us to tolerate too much of either. Without the body, when we are completely pure and free, not only is the pain boundless, but also the enjoyment and the pleasure. Moreover, just as the awareness of wrong becomes increasingly deep in Hell, the understanding and enjoyment of good grow constantly stronger in Paradise. Unlike Hell, which is a limited, finite stage, because it has to correct and amend what happened in a finite span of life, the joys of Paradise are endless and everlasting. To use a physical metaphor, the absolute zero of temperature is defined and closed; but there is no upper limit to higher and higher temperatures. The freed, cleansed soul is now able to have a touch of Godhead, which is the absolute infinity that contains the wholeness of everything. While being connected and confined by the body and by the shadows of the world, the soul can hardly grasp it, but in another stage of existence, when these boundaries are no longer there, the soul can keep ascending for eternity.[10]

‹⊖›

An adage attributed to several Jewish sages says, "Whoever is afraid of life is not afraid of death."

Envy

‹⊃

E n v y , a basic and quite common impulse, emerges very early. Even little children are full of envy; when a child sees that someone has something he wants, his first impulse seems to be to snatch it away. Obviously, envy does not end with childhood—we go on feeling it for a very long time, possibly to the end of our lives. The objects of our envy change as we grow; yet the nature of envy remains the same. As adults, we do not envy a little toy in someone's hand, but we may envy a fat bank account. In fact, envy is so pervasive that often we are either unaware of the feeling, or do not consider it a problem.

It seems that on the most primary level, envy—the green desire, as it used to be called—stems from a sense of deprivation: "Somebody else has it, and I don't; I want it, too." Most often, envy is possessive. It always seems to begin with simple desire for something—not so much because I want that thing, but because someone else has it. Often, this simple, childish possessiveness has very little to do with the object itself. A child in a toy store gets "big eyes," and wants to have all the playthings just because they are there, just because the shop has them, and not necessarily because he knows and wants each individual toy. Many people have had the experience of buying—either for a child or for an adult—a gift that was requested, even demanded—only to see it put aside once it is received. Often, it is never looked at again, because there was no real need for the thing itself. It was desirable just because someone else possessed it.

Envy is indiscriminate. Anything can be the object of envy: things that are useful or needed, things that are neither useful nor needed. Envy is not primarily focused on the object itself; it is prompted by the perceived status inherent in owning something that someone else owns, or that a particular social group considers a mark of distinction, of beauty, or of being "in."

Indeed, envied possessions or qualities often have little to do with what a person really wants; instead, they are related to where a person wants to be placed within society. In some primitive cultures, women knock out their front teeth or do other painful things in order to be considered beautiful. This may seem extreme to us, but one does not have to go very far to encounter such phenomena. In every physical fitness group, one can see men and women suffering in order to be what society considers acceptable or beautiful—even when it is not becoming for them, even when an emaciated person looks more like a scarecrow than like a model. The objective outcome of that physical fitness torture is immaterial, because it is not the way people really look that matters to them; rather, it is the way they fit into the social group. If fashion dictates that they have to look a certain way, then they will do so in order to "belong," even if in their hearts they dislike it.

Envy happens when we do not want to be deprived of what other people have. Beyond that, we want to have even what other people envy.

Sometimes, envy is satisfied simply when we own what others also have; in that case, the worst result may be a significant hole in one's pocket. I may want a bigger and fancier car not because I need it, but because someone else has it. The desire—sometimes turning into an obsession—to keep up with the Joneses is somehow appeased in the purchase of that car, or a better one.

But envy may develop in more negative, damaging ways. If I cannot have the object I envy, I may want to deprive the other of what he possesses. What happens when, by the very nature of the thing, it cannot be possessed by two people at the same time? Envy may then be transformed from a self-inflicted torment into an action to obtain what is desired. Lusting for someone else's ox, house, or wife is sinful, but not as sinful as actually maneuvering to get it. This is when envy turns into covetousness. Envy can be passive and quiet. Covetousness is envy that has matured from mere desire to action.

Furthermore, when the other has what I cannot have, the other is superior. When I deprive the other of what he has, we become equals again. If I cannot tolerate the fact that someone else is superior, this "equalization" is a source of great satisfaction. If I cannot attain his height, let me cut him down to my size.

I may even legally take something that belongs to another, but this does not make it any better morally. In a certain way, taking another's possessions with the assistance of a legal machinery may be even more despicable. These deeds cannot then be punished in a court of justice, and since their perpetrator is protected by the legal system, he is also protected from remorse.*

Envy may also acquire a public, political nature. In some cases "egalitarianism"—the moving force of some political movements—is just one of the ways of satisfying that spirit of envy: if I cannot have it, let no one have it. Inequality is intrinsic, whether due to inheritance, extremely hard work, or talent; not everyone can live in a

---

There is a story in the Talmud (Tractate Gittin 58a) about a man who used a number of legal tricks to deprive his friend of both his wife and his property; later, he married the woman and hired the former husband as his servant. Although this was all done in a perfectly legal manner, the Talmud states that this was the final evil deed that doomed the entire nation to destruction and exile.

palace, nor can everyone have a dream life. Envy makes us want to level all the differences, destroy all the palaces, make everyone's lives equally miserable.

The fact that so-and-so has what I want—a possession, an attribute, or a relationship—eats me up alive, does not allow me to sleep. After a while, I cease to care whether I possess it or not; I just want the other not to have it. I want the other destroyed, in order to stop my pain. This desire for destruction has nothing to do with the original object. At this point, it is not the object, but the other person's very existence that is threatening.

There is an ancient tale about two people, one of whom was envious of the other. The envious person was once given an opportunity to ask a favor from the King, with the proviso that his rival would get twice as much of whatever he requested. This put the envious person in a difficult position. After much consideration, he asked that one of his eyes be plucked out.

In a description of a visit to Hell, a group of people are seen sitting at a table, each with a bowl of soup and a spoon too long to bring the food to his own mouth. The only solution is for each to feed the person across from him; but because it is Hell, they all stay hungry forever. And we all know the famous judgment of Solomon (II Kings 3:16–28): two women gave birth, and one of the babies died; they both claimed to be the mother of the remaining child. To discover the truth, King Solomon suggested cutting the baby in two. The impostor gleefully accepted, saying: "It shall be neither yours nor mine; cut it!"

The spirit of envy feeds on itself and grows, changing eventually into a different emotion: one of pure hatred toward the envied person, a hatred that is never satisfied until it causes that person's destruction. In fact, it was said that all hatred can be cured except that which comes from envy.[1] The envied person cannot even appease the one who envies him, because the nicer and more generous he is, the more the other's envy will grow. The envious person will hate the other, not only for being richer or wiser, but also for being a better human being.

Some of the ugliest disputes about inheritance are motivated by envy that has turned into hatred. Often, they have nothing or little to do with the contents of the estate. While there may be plenty for everyone, some people simply cannot endure the notion that someone else might have more than they. Fights of this kind can continue for years—between nations, even for hundreds of years—and perhaps never come to a conclusion. They are not really fights over material possessions; it is the pure spirit of envy that grows, that devours, that becomes a power unto itself. Such a vendetta, waiting for the downfall of the other party, can become a person's sole raison d'être, so much so that if such a person succeeds, life suddenly becomes meaningless.

Thus, whether or not envy is successful, it is destructive for all involved, including the envious person. The envious person is not necessarily a danger to others; not everyone is capable of turning thought and desire into actual deed, or of causing actual harm. It is also possible that the envious person, however dark his thoughts and desires may be, is restrained by morality or by law. Invariably, though, even when it does not come to fruition, envy destroys the person who harbors it.

Although envy is usually considered purely negative, like so many other things, it is not unequivocally so. Envy creates big industries; in fact, the industries of envy are as big, or perhaps bigger, than the industries of need. Two salient examples are the car and fashion industries. The more developed a country is, the more resources it devotes to the industries of envy. It uses all available means to create new needs—through direct and indirect advertising, propaganda, and so on—and then goes on to create things designed to fulfill those newly created needs.

Though often destructive and ugly, envy may also stimulate great and beautiful things. Maimonides says that had it not been for the crazy and envious people, the world would not be built.[2] He describes how people spend their lives working hard, continually endangering themselves in order to build, say, beautiful villas that will last for hundreds of years, while they themselves may survive to enjoy them only for a very short time.

Envy is also closely connected with the competitive urge, an urge that is sometimes even stronger than the desire for the thing itself. When people compete with others, they do better than if they were doing the same thing on their own. Competition gives rise to the drive to outdo, to outgrow, or to outmaneuver, to be higher, richer, stronger. That drive is well known and is used—sometimes officially and legally, sometimes unofficially and illegally—in competitive sports: often, what makes Sammy run is that Morris is running, too. The desire for victory is even stronger than the will to achieve. It is a very powerful, almost subconscious motivational force.

Competitiveness also exists among animals; "King of the Hill" is a game that even little kittens know, and it is not the hill that matters, but who is on top. Even the natural forces themselves—fire and water, heaven and earth—can be depicted as being in envious competition with each other.[3] From what we know about angels, it seems that even among them there exists some rivalry and jealousy.[4]

Envy cannot and ought not to be ignored; but it can be utilized for good. Our sages say that all envy is bad, except the envy of scholars, *Kinat Soferim.*[5] This kind of envy can inspire a person to attain a higher level. The same sort of competitiveness that can be seen in sports, or in the desire to obtain material possessions, can also apply to nonmaterial possessions such as wisdom, knowledge, even saintliness.

As odd as it may seem, a person's envy of spiritual superiority, and the desire not just to imitate, but to outdo, can become a creative, growth-inducing power. Universities, think tanks, and symposia that bring scholars together use this inner mechanism to generate intellectual growth. A fair amount of philanthropy, too, comes from competition and envy. Competition of this sort may create a certain amount of greatness. There is, of course, a touch—sometimes more than a touch—of ego here, but altogether, the outcome is positive.

The Book of Proverbs (23:17) says, "Do not be envious of the wicked, but be envious of the fear of God." It seems that we are born with a big container full of desires. We cannot get rid of them, nor must we. Rather, our problem and our task is to discern what to do with our emotions and our attributes. We can use our emotions either as building blocks that may become the ingredients of our spiritual growth, or as harmful, disruptive elements that will destroy both ourselves and others. We are possibly envious by nature; however, we have free will, and can choose the objects of our envy. Thus, we can be envious of a wicked person and want to outdo him in his wickedness—or we can look up to people who are better than we are: nicer, nobler, doing more good deeds. If it is they whom I aspire to outdo, then I grow spiritually.

Unfortunately, however, people usually put their envy to lower, rather than higher, causes. People tend to envy those who have more than they materially, and feel very complacent when comparing themselves to those who are spiritually less lucky, or less equipped. They think, "Well, I am not a criminal like so-and-so, I am a pretty good person"; and then they go on tormenting themselves, saying, "If I am so good, why does this fellow have a car one yard longer than mine?" Instead, we should compare ourselves with those who have less materially, but more spiritually. Moreover, like a person who is too proud to sin, we, too, can decide not to allow the ugly sort of envy to rule us. We can decide that such a lowly emotion is unbecoming for us, that it is beneath our dignity.

This is not just the difference between the material and the spiritual, between the noble and the base. Envying the good in someone else does not make us want to take that away from him.* Although the driving power of this kind of envy is ego, it is an ego sublimated. The purity and nobility of the desire may be debatable; yet when envy drives people to achieve more, or to improve themselves, then that base desire becomes a motivating force that can make the world a better place.†

Let us end with a story, a true one, about positive envy. The great Hassidic Rebbe known as "the Holy Jew"[6] said that he owed his great achievements to a blacksmith. In his youth, he lived next to a diligent blacksmith who would begin working very early every morning. When the

---

Even in this realm, however, evil may penetrate. Scholarly and even saintly envy may turn to attaining higher social status by trying to belittle the superior person, in order to be perceived as better or wiser than the other; see, for example, Maimonides, Mishneh Torah, Sefer ha-Mada', Hilkhot De'ot 6:4.

†The opposite of envy is self-satisfaction. Our sages (in Pirkei Avot, "The Ethics of Our Fathers," 4:1) praise the one who is content with what he has. However, self-satisfaction, too, can be a two-edged sword. Someone who is satisfied with his share will not be driven to do evil, but he may stagnate because he will not be driven to creativity either.*

Holy Jew heard him work, he would say to himself, "This man is just working for money; I am studying Torah, which is much higher and nobler. If he can deprive himself of sleep, and rise to work so early, how can it be that I cannot get up at that time?" He then began to rise for his study a little bit earlier. The blacksmith heard the Holy Jew studying aloud, and he thought to himself, "I work for my livelihood, but this young man does not earn anything for his studies. If he can rise this early, then I can rise even earlier." So he did. The Holy Jew then started a little bit earlier, and they went on competing in this way for quite a while. The Holy Jew then said that the competition gained him so much time that he was able to achieve greatness.

In this competition, neither the Holy Jew nor the blacksmith lost anything; both only gained. They used the spirit of envy to find a common measure—their use of time—and competed about using that time for doing the work they wanted to do. This envy created a spirit of rivalry, a desire for victory, the urge to be uppermost, and it spurred two people, in different walks of life and in different realms, into doing more—each in his own way.

Hollywood

❧

Hollywood is not just a place—it is a world in itself. Hollywood has done something remarkable: it has created a great and very successful religion. Through its successful missionaries—the films produced in Hollywood—it has spread all around the globe, gaining adherents faster than any other religion in the world. If it has not attained the stature of a full-fledged religion, at least it is a very strong cult.

Hollywood films are, of course, also a business, an amusement, and a highly efficient means for whiling away—even killing—as much time as anyone might want to kill. However, in this regard, it is not very different from other businesses or other parts of the amusement industry. Hollywood does much more than kill time, though. Holly-

wood has a formative influence on people's lives. Hollywood influences people's thinking, their values, their
goals, the way they plan their lives, and their behavior.
That is why boys will imitate the stance and language of a
star, and girls will spend their last dollars just to have a
Hollywood-style wedding.

Beyond that, Hollywood creates images of this world
and of the next world; it creates desire and it creates
dreams. Whether these dreams are far-fetched and unattainable, or very close to reality, they become the dreams
of the people; they are the wishes of the people. People
copy the manners, the behavior, the images, and the figures that Hollywood creates. In that sense, it is as powerful and as meaningful as any religion.

Like most religions and cults, it has both idols and
worshippers, and a hierarchy not unlike that of a church.
Its leaders do not have glorious titles such as Archbishop
or Grand Lama, settling instead on being executives, producers, and directors. Even so, the lack of high-sounding
titles and fancy dress does not hamper them from being
rulers—sometimes absolute rulers—of their world. Like a
church, Hollywood has active and passive members; some
people make the rules, and others comply with them.
There are the acolytes and the priests of the cult, and the
multitude of worshippers.

Hollywood is a syncretistic religion that mixes pagan,
Christian, and uniquely Hollywood elements. It is not
new, or particularly creative. It recasts traditional images
and elements in its own image in order to convey its message. The pagan elements are clearly apparent. This reli-

gion does not have one particular "prophet," such as Moses or Muhammad, who could unanimously be considered its founder. Instead, it has a fair number of creators, some of whom have been identified, while others are left as hazy memories. The Hollywood pantheon contains the same gods of ancient times: Baal-Jupiter, the high god who became the god of money and power; Mars-Udin, who became the fierce fighter and soldier; Venus-Astarte, the goddess of fertility (and, nowadays, mostly of sex). These, and their minor helpers, are the abstract gods; their embodiments are the Movie Stars, who are mythic figures.

Like the ancient idols, some of the movie idols do not see, do not hear, do not feel anything. They are just bodies, images manipulated by producers and directors, the high priests of the Hollywood religion, who preach the gospel. These mini-gods, the stars, are worshipped. They are the subjects of dreams. Fans hang, and even kiss, pictures and posters of movie stars, and are enraptured when they can see them close up or even touch them. Their worshippers—as well as the worshippers of rock singers—create riots that are just like the riotous bacchanalia of earlier times.

Like many ancient religions—Egyptian, Babylonian, or Greek—the Hollywood religion does not have a clear-cut message or mission; it just exists. The tenets of this religion are not very explicit. It has many principles, most of them unwritten—there is no Holy Book of Hollywood. In that sense, too, it is similar to many primitive, ancient, and strong religions all over the world. These cults do not have a holy scripture, a book of law or theology, but they do have very clear-cut forms of worship, as well as principles and ways of behavior.

Like Christianity—especially Protestantism—the Hollywood religion is very concerned with intention, sentiment, and emotion. The deed is of secondary importance. Within certain limits, the proper emotion justifies any outcome. It is the hero's good intentions that matter; how he reaches his goal is far less important. The benevolent thief, the kindhearted prostitute, the noble killer can, and do, become heroes. Nevertheless, the Hollywood hero, unlike the villain, is not entirely free of boundaries. The Hollywood religion actually has a fairly limited framework, and cannot tolerate things or people that are too far outside that framework. Its internal moral code dictates that certain crimes are always punished. However, if you mean well, if you are in love, if you are a patriot, or if you are a victim—as long as your heart is pure, all the rest is not really very important.

The Hollywood religion is also a great believer in the happy ending, and in this it resembles some of the world's greatest religions, such as Judaism, Christianity, and Islam. However, unlike these religions, Hollywood simplifies the message. Its happy endings arrive faster (they must come at the end of the movie), and are far less connected to past deeds—except, of course, for the "pure heart." Hollywood conveys the message that the world is like a fairy tale: somehow, it will all work out well in the end.

There are adventures and adversities, ups and downs, but these are, basically, like those in an amusement park. You do not ride the roller coaster or the Ferris wheel with the notion that you might fall and be hurt, or possibly die. You are able to enjoy the thrill because you have the firm conviction that you will always land safely. It may take a very long time and it may be quite complicated, but there will be, there must always be, a happy ending. The bad guys will ultimately be defeated and destroyed; the good guys will win and be happy. The story can be emotionally moving in other places, but the end has to be not only positive, it has to be happy. Often, the end is not just a solution to the problem—it has to be a happy solution. Even when the happy ending is not built into the story— some stories just cannot have a happy end, and the source material does not contain one—the Hollywood version will end happily, because otherwise it would be sacrilegious.

In this, the Hollywood religion diverges from pagan religions, which are far less interested in morality, allow for a great deal of real cruelty, and do not believe in happy endings.* The Greek tragedies have no solution and no happy ending; some of them even end with everything destroyed and everyone killed. Hollywood does not accept such negativity, and not just because people do not like it. Such tragedy is contrary to Hollywood's basic message.

Many pagan religions have a rather pessimistic view of the end, and believe that ultimately, in the end of days, the world will be destroyed. The Nordic gods and the Greek gods were mortal, and inherently incapable of solving all the problems; their myths were saturated with cruelty and full of unresolved conflict.

What is the main point of the Hollywood religion? It is not sex. Although there is always a certain amount of sex mixed into the story, and very few Hollywood productions are completely devoid of anything sexual, sex is not the main tenet. As in many pagan religions, sex is one of the main rites. However, the Hollywood moral code dictates that this sex happen within a framework of love, even if it is a hollow image of love. Even in the more depraved productions, sex conveys at least some external, superficial resemblance to love. Anyone who has "clinical," purely loveless, sex is obviously the villain. In any case, even when the sex is blatantly clear, it is not an aim in itself. Sex conveys the charm of the hero, or is the reward he receives for his success.

The main tenet of Hollywoodism can be summed up in one word: happiness. Happiness is the goal, the aim, the motivation for anything and everything. For some people, happiness may be sitting alone and looking at a tree, and for others it is hard work done well, but those are surely not examples of Hollywood-style happiness. Hollywood's definition of happiness is comfort. It is a this-worldly happiness, not a heavenly happiness or a feeling of supernal bliss. The material goods, the house, the lifestyle, the dress are the happy endings of strife and struggle. Success is defined materially, and achievement is defined as gaining more of that brand of worldly happiness. The motivation behind every Hollywood story is the pursuit of happiness—which is, of course, attained at the happy end.

All these elements put together, coupled with the de-

sire to reach as many people as possible,* create another
important aspect of Hollywood: the glorification of mediocrity. Outstanding achievements, in any field, are not
part of the Hollywood religion. The Hollywood dream is
not to be on top of the world, nor is it a goal to have great
affluence, fame, or fortune. The outstanding people, of
any kind, are not the real heroes. They may be part of the
background scene, but are never supposed to be the objective of one's striving. The goal is to be in a comfortable
position, within the usual range. Excellence is just not
within the doctrine of this particular religion.

The Hollywood dream is to be a successful mediocre
person. Hollywood glorifies neither geniuses nor fools; it
venerates ordinary people. Even outstanding historical
figures are shrunk down to size, to be more or less the
same as everybody else, within the limits of the main-
stream. Hollywood makes the mediocre person feel that
the hero is like himself in his daydreams—stronger,
slightly cleverer, handsomer, sometimes even endowed
with some supernatural powers, but behind all these dis-
guises, the hero is really just a successful Everyman.

Very much like the Greek gods, the Hollywood-style heroes are ordinary human beings, not too outstanding, intrinsically not too much of anything, but with some
exaggerated prowess, underneath which they are cast in a
human mold. They are glorified simple people, glorified

*There is obvious financial motivation for that, but it also has
to do with the desire to be liked, to be popular.*

mediocre people. The striking beauty should be a beautiful version of the boy or girl next door. Therefore, Hollywood-style beauty occurs always within a certain range of normalcy. Outstanding, startling beauties—Modigliani or Rubens types, for instance—will not work in Hollywood. The Hollywood hero has to be the simple person glorified, yet still within the norm.

These rules are true in all types of filmmaking. These rules even hold true for Disney cartoons, which, even though they do not have human stars, use the same images. Cartoon characters are created in exactly the same mold as the human stars; in fact, because they are more simplified, they are better. *Aladdin* is a very nice example of this: a little bit of miracle, a little bit of humor—but not too much; everything is so very nice and sweet, and very well packaged. There is not much difference between Aladdin and Bambi—they even have the same eyes.

The Hollywood message, then, is to create for people a well-planned, technically superb daydream, which says softly, "I am all right, you are all right, basically, with small aberrations here and there, everything will be all right." It hints, "You, too, are a hero. Look at these stars: in your inner heart, you are almost like them. Perhaps you are not as handsome, nor as strong, but you can dream about being like them."

This religion does not demand anything exceptional from its followers, even as viewers. The messages and images created by Hollywood are not necessarily bad, but they all have shallowness built in. Shallowness is intrinsic; everything has to be within the audience's grasp, tailored to its level of understanding, as well as to its dreams. Hollywood could not make a good movie about a saint—or a scientist or an artist—because a real saint, by definition, would not be within the norm. A saint is not part of normal society. He is an outsider, and is not, nor can he be, "me." Therefore, good—however it may be depicted—is never very good, because if it were very good, we would not be able to identify with it without changing a lot within ourselves.

Hollywood functions in the same way as an advertising campaign—advertising itself and the American spirit. Very often, advertising is the best, most interesting, and most creative part of many magazines; to market something properly takes a lot of thought. Whether it says so explicitly or not, an ad implies, "If you buy this dress, you will be as beautiful as the model wearing it." In actuality, the model may be just as beautiful without the dress, and most purchasers of the dress will not become as beautiful as the model even when wearing the dress.

Like any effective advertising campaign, Hollywood is very professional and very good at achieving its aim. It is so successful that it creates a world. It creates imitations, dreams, and people who want to live the Hollywood lifestyle, which is a crude representation of the "American spirit." Beyond that, America and Hollywood have a reciprocal relationship: Hollywood draws from within America and simultaneously re-creates America in its own image. Hollywood does not draw an image from one particular segment of society; its image distills a fundamental national sense of optimism. Hollywood depicts an amusement park world, addressed to a democratic audience. The audience of the show is important to Hollywood not only because it pays for the tickets and thus finances the religion. The audience is something far bigger: it is, itself, the dream and the image.

In this sense, Hollywood is an advertisement for a dream, a very shallow dream—a dream about a simplified Heaven, about life that is supposed to be reality, but is not. For life is not like the movies. In how many Hollywood pictures do you see a person cleaning a house or washing a baby—especially a really dirty baby? In the Hollywood world, you see the results, but you do not see the sweat; you do not see the hard work. And think how different real relationships are from the way people fall in love in the movies. We all know that life does not always happen according to Hollywood pictures; still, some part of us believes that they are pictures of a possible reality. Hollywood has trained us to believe that somehow there will be a happy end, and that if something in real life does not work out, it is just a mishap. Therefore, we do not distrust the Hollywood religion itself. We tend to think that if something goes wrong, it is our fault—we were doing it wrong in the first place, or it was not the right solution. Even in those few movies that leave us unhappy, we somehow think that this unhappiness is incidental, it is not that important. We believe that the misery will somehow be resolved by itself, by a hero, or by good luck, and that it will surely pass. People know that those are dreams, but they believe that they can

somehow become real. In that sense, the Hollywood religion
is the "opiate of the masses."

Being a very self-satisfied religion, Hollywood is not
revolutionary; it is even anti-revolutionary. For one thing,
Hollywood does not try to change norms, and certainly
does not have the presumption to steer them; it merely reflects existing ones. When actors, or film heroes, behave
in ways that were unthinkable or unspeakable years ago,
it is simply because the general social norms have
changed. Hollywood glorifies the status quo, or at least
promotes the dreams of Middle America as the best of all
possible worlds, and thereby diminishes the possibility for
change.

Almost every revolutionary movement in recent times
has had some messianic vision of how to change the
world, to make it into a better place. The truly revolutionary vision must include the notion of strife, of struggle, of problems that are not easy to solve, and of suffering
that is not immediately ameliorated. These are not
themes that Hollywood wants to deal with. Hollywood
does not produce revolutionary films or portray the true
misery of the world. Although it does occasionally depict
suffering, it does not show many real tragedies, and no
deep or revolutionary change is portrayed.*

The Hollywood make-believe dream lies in the eye of
the beholder, the viewer in a movie theater or home

**Even a revolutionary theme is toned down in Hollywood. In
Cecil B. DeMille's film* The Ten Commandments, *Moses
and even God are made over in the Hollywood form.*

watching TV, and believing. The Hollywood religion is very successful, and has permeated the general culture so much, that everybody half-believes the fantasy—but half-belief is enough for this kind of religion, because the basic message is so very persuasive and moving.

These characteristics make the Hollywood religion strong enough to undermine, and even destroy, many existing religious forms and cults. For instance, it is quite possible that Hollywood played a more powerful role in destroying the Soviet regime than all the military vehicles of the United States. The Hollywood dream slipped through small gaps in the Iron Curtain—it was not considered dangerous, but it created a new world, not only by showing the existence of a different, more comfortable world, but mostly by replacing even the Soviet vision of the future with the Hollywood dreamworld, dreams of mediocrity, comfort, and the simplest material forms of happiness.

It is possible that the Hollywood religion, like many others, will die one day. Of course, Hollywood as an actual place may diminish in size, or move to a different site, but that does not mean that Hollywood as an idea will be destroyed. As it stands now, it is very well established, deeply woven into the fabric of reality, supplying daydreams to the world.

Masks

⟿

S i n c e earliest times, actors have used theater masks—
the comic mask and the tragic mask—but the masks of
normal human behavior are far more common. These
masks are symbols of the parts we play in the drama of
life. We may play one role at one time, and another role at
another, but we wear masks almost all the time. We humans are never completely naked.[1]

Our masks change as we develop through the stages of
life. Once we are grown, we wear professional masks at
work; at home, we wear the mask of a parent, a spouse.
Some masks include a complete change of attire. In fact,
almost all attire is a mask, implying a role. I am an enticing young lady. I am a serious person. I am going on a
business trip, on a hunt, for a leisurely stroll. In each

case, I wear the proper dress for that occasion. My attire proclaims what I am: now I am a businessperson, now I am a nymph. The soldier, the police officer, the corporate executive, and the street sweeper all dress for their parts.

Not only do we change masks for the various activities of our daily lives, we also change masks with different people. We have many masks, and we are capable of changing them remarkably fast. Every time we undergo a conscious or unconscious shift of roles, we—symbolically—change masks. With one friend, I am a certain person; I wear a certain mask. With another person, I wear a different mask. Some people are extremely good at making that shift. You may have seen people, at a party for instance, changing masks at lightning speed. Someone can be one kind of a person, then turn to speak to somebody else and immediately play a very different role. Watching a good social mixer in a diverse group is like watching a great actor making instant role changes. People also react differently to the same person at different times. If you watch carefully, you can see people move through society wearing and shedding masks fiercely. Sometimes the differences are subtle; sometimes they are clear, strong, abrupt changes—in which you can see the serious person, the joker, the loving person, the cynic, the enthusiast.

Some of our masks are put on consciously; we wear social smiles at parties, sad faces at funerals, laugh at unamusing jokes, and pretend to listen attentively when our minds are completely elsewhere. Of course, some of our facial expressions are unconscious and spontaneous; we may smile because we are genuinely happy, and cry because we are sad. Even so, many of our facial expressions and involuntary movements are not instinctive and inborn, but acquired (albeit at a very early age) by imitation. Indeed, some of the simplest forms of expression, such as nodding an assent, are not universal but customs of a particular society. It is astonishing to see the vast collection of masks most people have—maybe thousands!

Mask-wearing is ingrained in us from the moment of birth. From early infancy, long before they learn to talk, children cry not because of pain, but in order to get attention, smile to ingratiate themselves to others, and generally, show off. From childhood, we are taught to speak politely to some people, because that is part of the human relationship. Social pressures make us behave politely. We cannot kick everyone that we dislike in the face. Similarly, we cannot express love to everybody that we are in love with—again, because of social conventions. As well as wearing, at times, the comic mask and the tragic mask, we also wear masks of boredom or indifference. "The stiff upper lip" of one society is a mask, no less than the giggling of another.

We are accustomed to being stage-dressed with each other: we are dressed in manners as well as in clothes. We are dressed, so we address each other, "Excuse me, Mr. So-and-So." "How do you do?" "Please." "Thank you." "Have a nice day." All these phrases are the dresses of politeness. The precisely calculated formal bow is a part of Japanese society, while slaps on the back and rough jokes seem to fulfill the same function in another.

Though we are not always aware of it, society—a different aspect of society—also puts pressure on people to pretend that they are much worse than they really are. We sometimes acquire façades, masks of demons, in order to be allowed to enter certain societies. In some warlike cultures (or groups), people have to be harsh, arrogant, and cruel to be socially acceptable. In the same way, sophisticated society demands that we be witty, dishonest, and critical.[2]

Wearing a mask is not only a way of being integrated within a wide society, but also a device used in close, even intimate relationships. Years ago, a young woman came to me just before her wedding to ask a rather practical question about her marriage. The young woman had recently become an observant Jew, but mentally and emotionally she belonged to the 1960s. We somehow entered into a long discussion about life and about her picture of married life. Because she was one of the flower children, she had a vision of an ideal life that would be based on complete frankness and openness. I told her—which may not seem like proper rabbinical advice*—that being married is not like being in court; you are not swearing to tell the truth, the whole truth, and nothing but the truth. You don't need to make a full clinical revelation of all your past experiences; some things you can skip. About half a year later, I met her husband, and it was obvious that she

---

In fact, however, it really was properly rabbinical; see Babylonian Talmud, Tractate Yevamot 65b.

had not listened. It was clear how hurtful that was. She not only told the truth about what she thought of him at any given moment, but also about her past life. I could see that the man could not bear so much truth.

The positive power of a mask is that it is sometimes protection for the self, and in other cases, it is protection for others. In order to maintain a social life and to be a caring person who is not destructive, we have to wear masks. It is possible to kill a person by saying something in a short, curt, naked way, or to spare someone by conveying exactly the same information in a different format, covered in wraps that make it bearable.

Our masks perform a wide range of functions, and taking them off may be dangerous. We wear masks for protection. Sometimes the mask is a dress, sometimes it is a shield, sometimes we protect ourselves with thick iron armor. When a person lives near one of the polar circles, it is obviously necessary to wear clothes in order to exist. Being dressed, being covered, is a simple existential need. Undressing in the street and on the beach is almost as dangerous—we now know—as being naked at the North Pole. It is as necessary to protect the body against harm from great heat or abundant sunshine as from the harm of great cold. Physiological undressing and psychological undressing are connected. Both physically and psychologically, wearing a mask, a dress, a cover, can be superior to full exposure because it is protection for the being. It is not a lie, but a shield. It is a part of what we have to do in order to survive.

Although we all wear masks, at most times, we also know that they are only masks, that in a way, none of them is real. When we put on a mask, is that a deliberate falsification? What is the relationship between the person and the mask? The term "mask" implies more than just a simple interaction. The mask reveals and hides simultaneously. In a certain way, every word is the mask of an idea, revealing and hiding at the same time. The relationship between the naked self—if there is such a thing—and its masks is therefore always intricate and complex.

The fact that we are aware of our masks is, in itself, part of what we are. We are not dumb creatures; we are conscious beings, making choices about our masks. However, these choices are also a reflection of what is inside. Some people are hypocritical or deceptive without realizing it, but even when people are knowingly, clearly, intentionally hypocritical, the sham is never complete. In some way, whether the person dons the mask unconsciously or consciously, inadvertently or willfully, the mask is never entirely foreign. We put on a mask as if it were external, but somehow it comes from within us, even when we think we are imitating someone else. The choices we make about how we appear are as important as what we are without appearances, if one can imagine such a thing. No matter how deliberate we think the choice of a mask may be, it inevitably reflects some truth about the self behind the mask.

Because our masks are the result of an ongoing process of change—with age, time, and society—we do not have rigid, external masks; we have masks that grow from within us. Where does this shell stop, and where does the creature begin? Is the tortoise's shell a house? Is it a defense? Is it a mask? Can you imagine the tortoise without its shell? It is part of the tortoise. Of course, there is a difference: although the tortoise creates the shell, it cannot change it at will. We humans are far more complex, and so we can—and do—change masks. However, in every form, in every change, we are creating something from within ourselves. At the same time that we are creating the mask, the mask is also creating the person behind it. Fiction stories have been written about how, if you live long enough with a mask, when you take it off, you find that your face bears a resemblance to the mask,[3] even if you no longer want it. Our masks are not just simple external shells, but something that both grows from within, and creates us. We create, and we are created.

We can change masks, but is it possible to get rid of the mask altogether? If we are capable of changing masks, then there must be a "self" capable of taking off one mask and then putting on another. Can this "self" actually be completely naked, entirely "itself"? Sometimes, this undressing is just the act of putting on another form, another dress, a different mask. I may think that I can see more of the "real" so-and-so in the bedroom than in the boardroom; but that idea falls apart when you examine what people actually do. People play roles everywhere. They may play roles only in a group of well-dressed people, or they may play roles naked in bed—though different roles, indeed. It is a different mask, but still a mask. I can decide, "I will no longer be Little Lord Fauntleroy, I will be Tarzan of the Apes," but no matter the mask, it is still a mask. The basic premise of role-playing has not changed. In truth, we never seem to get rid of masks entirely.

In many cultures, there is a horror of undressing physically, but everywhere there is the much deeper fear of undressing spiritually. We feel that there are many ugly things inside us; some of these are evil and frightening, some are soft spots or ridiculous, stupid things. So we go on playing a role, afraid to divest ourselves of the role and reveal what is inside. Living, growing, and learning add layers to one's natural existence. These are built like the shell of an oyster, or the layers of an onion. What is the real onion? You can peel away one layer after another; what will remain in the end? Perhaps our whole existence is like an onion—multiple layers, one inside the other. Perhaps the horror of undressing is the fear that, like the onion, when all the layers are peeled away, nothing will be left.

On the other hand, we also want to undress. The warrior coming home wants to take off his armor, the businessman, his tie and jacket. Similarly, we may feel tired of being "dressed" in so many covers of politeness or respectability, and yearn to expose those parts within the external layers. By revealing the hidden parts, we think we become lighter, freer, even happier. If we were able to take off the masks of culture or education, we would become more true to ourselves. This feeling is based on the assumption that simple or primitive people are more truthful, authentic, or uncontrived. Is it so? If it were feasible to take off the mask, would it reveal a greater truth? Is the naked person—the person without a mask—in some way more honest or more natural than the person with a mask? Is the mask part of our identity more artificial, or is it as important an aspect of ourselves, of our persona, as those parts that are known only to ourselves? Is the naked person any barer than the well-dressed gentleman? Is the "real Adam" the naked one, or the dressed one?

Now, what happens when people take off these dresses, and speak their mind? Let us put it in more picturesque language, just to make the question starker. Suppose I meet someone, and I say, "I really want to see you as you are; undress!" So the fellow undresses, until he is completely naked. Then I say, "But you are still dressed. Strip off your flesh. Get down to the real substance. Let's get down to the skeleton." Is the skeleton more real than the full-fleshed body? If I get to the bone, have I gotten to truth? Is that the person? Do we see more of the "real person"? Or is it possibly only a partial, incorrect image?

There are many other parts, other layers even deeper than bone. Is a person undergoing Freudian analysis really getting to the truth? Stripping away all the layers does not necessarily reveal a truer self, just a different one, made to a Freudian measure. It is still only a partial reality. When a small child learns the art of undressing a doll, he undresses all the dolls. Then he tries to undress the dog. Maybe children have pure scientific curiosity—they want to see the truth; they want to see what makes things tick.

What is behind this metaphor? What is the truest part of a person? Is the apparel that we put on later inferior to that which we had at birth? Are the coverings that we put on later in life any less genuine than the grunt, the wordless cry? If a person is stripped, not only of flesh, but of all life's acquisitions—culture, language, thoughts, dreams, ideas—down to the level of pure spirit, that will still not distill the essence of the person. Pure spirit is another kind of skeleton, but it is not self. The person is also his connection to all these outer layers. The biological body and the emotional body, all those things that are generated from within, as well as all those masks that are acquired from others by willful imitation, become part of the feeling of self. The self is a combination, and this combined entity contains flesh, blood, feelings, mind, spirit, soul—and the person also includes the masks.

An abstract, clean-cut, primal nature, a true self, possibly does not exist at all. Finding the true self is not just a question of whether it is possible to undress completely, or whether undressing reveals a greater truth; there is also a need to understand whether this undressing is any kind of an achievement. Is the creature who was stripped of everything better? Is a person who reveals naked, shameless desire superior? Should passion be sublimated, to use Freud's expression? Should it be changed and dressed? Is that changed, dressed, more formal creature not superior to the other one?

One story that deals with this complex notion is the story of an encounter between Rabbi Akiva and the Roman ruler of Palestine, Tinneus Rufus (whom the Jews nicknamed Tyrannus Rufus).* The two leaders had a philosophical dispute, which on the one hand was connected with the spiritual collapse of paganism in Rome itself, and on the other, with the political friction between the Jewish population and the Roman rulers.

The Roman asked Rabbi Akiva which is superior: nature, or what people make of it—that is, what God does, or the handicraft of man. Rabbi Akiva immediately answered, "What humans do is superior to what God does." So the Roman asked, "Can man create Heaven and earth?" "No," said Akiva, "we cannot create Heaven and earth, but when we speak about things that human beings can do, we do it better. Look at a stalk of flax on the one hand, and the piece of linen cloth that is made from it; look at a sheaf of wheat, and look at a loaf of bread. Which is superior?" When the Roman came to this impasse, he asked, "Tell me, why are you circumcised?" So Akiva answered, "I told you, what man does is better than what God does."

*This happened around the year 130 C.E., prior to the Bar Kochba Revolt against the Romans. Rabbi Akiva was one of the greatest Jewish scholars of his age, and, in fact, of all ages. Tinneus Rufus did not win the argument; he finished it later on by ordering that Rabbi Akiva be put to death.

Tinneus Rufus wanted to make the point that the natural world is superior, thus negating one of the basic premises of Judaism, that humans, too, bear a responsibility for this world, and that they are supposed, and even commanded, to make it better. Rabbi Akiva did not allow him to develop his idea. The Rabbi was not making a joke, nor was his just a tactical move. Rabbi Akiva's stance has broad implications. The natural object is not necessarily the superior object. The natural creature itself, the naked creature, is not always the superior creature. The human that is dressed, and is therefore masked, is a different creature, and in some ways, a superior one.

The Biblical commandment to the priests, "And you shall make them linen breeches to cover their nakedness" (Exodus 28:42), is not intended to command a form of modesty, so that other people do not see the priests' private parts, since they wore long shirts down to their ankles. It seems, therefore, that this covering was intended to cover the priests' nakedness from themselves.

Symbolically, this cover, which is necessary for the ritual, has a psychological meaning as well. There are parts of the self that had better not be exposed, not even to oneself. Imposing on people to expose and reveal hidden parts may not be a positive move. Dressing does not make these parts disappear; they are still there. However, uncovering them, examining them continuously, is harmful. There are points in everyone that should be covered, because constant inspection makes them more powerful and compelling, even overwhelming. The amount of hidden, unconscious vice in anyone is tremendous. As long as these parts of the self are hidden, one can somehow deal with them. Once they are apparent, they tilt the balance of the self; they become far more threatening when they are in the open. The French philosopher Montaigne wrote that if people were to be punished for their thoughts, everyone would deserve hanging several times every day.

This repression is not just a defense mechanism against outsiders; it also defends people against themselves. There is an Aramaic expression, "What the heart does not reveal to the mouth."[4] Likewise, there are things that the heart does not reveal even to itself. Only exceptional people have the power to look into the chasms of their soul. Opening them may be like opening the crust of a lava-filled fissure—the fiery matter may erupt and destroy everything.

Thus, this cover of internal chastity, this inner mask, is a shield for self-protection. Opening it should be done with extreme caution, and in very special times. ("The heart is deceitful above all things and desperately wicked; who can know it?" Jeremiah 17:9.) God knows it anyway; other people may suspect it—but it is better not to have a full view. Covering it is not deceit, but rather a way of containing and controlling it. One should try to integrate these parts, mend them, use them wisely—but first try to keep this den of fierce, ferocious things properly circumscribed.

In a discourse on charity, the sages turn to the case of those who do not need alms, yet pretend that they do.[5]

They say that if a person pretends to be lame, and asks for charity as a lame person, he will not die until he becomes lame. If a person pretends to have a certain disease, he will not die until he gets it. The lie will become true. The mask will become reality. Even against one's will, the mask exercises a huge power over the person. In a later period, somebody asked, "That is what happens when one pretends to be lame; what if someone pretends to be a saint?" The answer is the same: he will not die until he becomes a saint; that will be his punishment. It is a punishment, because the life of a saint is so much harder than that of the hypocrite. Yet it is also a reward—for having assumed this particular mask.

The Midrash says that on Mount Sinai, God appeared to each person according to his or her individual understanding.[6] The Jewish definition of leadership is the ability to react to each person in a different way. Perhaps it is a Divine gift to be able to appear different to each person, according to his or her need.

Perhaps the real question is not whether a person can or should undress, but rather, what is the best mask to wear. Is one mask superior to another? What is the best way in which to dress my identity so it will seem more elevated? The human being and the dress, the nature and the artifact, the human hand and the tool are all intricately interconnected.

Our unique nature, then, is in our capacity to choose our mask: the demon or the angel.

Friends

❧

T h e term "friendship" does not have an exact, universal meaning. Its precise definition may be, like pornography, a matter of geography, and indeed, its meaning varies from country to country and from culture to culture. Everyone agrees that a friend is somebody who is not an enemy, or, if you prefer, who is the opposite of an enemy; but outside that negative definition, "friendship" covers a wide range of relationships.

In some countries, where the word "friend" is used very loosely, a person sitting next to me in a coffee shop, or a colleague at work, might be called a friend, whereas in other countries such a person would be considered barely an acquaintance. Our own understanding of the word "friend" is so vague that in English "boyfriend" or "girlfriend" can refer to a relationship that may not be a friendship at all. In other countries, such as Russia—and this has more to do with deep cultural norms than with the social or political system—friends are taken far more seriously, and friendship implies a deep emotional tie, more important than any other relationship, transcending even close family ties. People may change spouses six or seven times, but a friendship can last for life.

In modern English, there is no linguistic distinction between "you" plural and "you" singular. In French, German, Russian, and many other languages, using the honorific, plural "you"* to address an equal or a superior establishes and expresses a formal relationship, and the singular, familiar "you" is reserved mainly for close friendships and family. The shift from the you-plural into the distinctly different you-singular marks a change in the relationship from formal to intimate. In many European countries, people marked this shift from formal to intimate language in a ceremonious way, sometimes fixed by custom. It may be done in a lighthearted way or very seriously, but it always contains some celebration, because it signifies a change from a formal or commonplace relationship into closeness and intimacy.

This linguistic distinction highlights the fact that friendship goes far beyond a word that can be used indis-

---

For example: Vous (plural) and tu (singular) in French; sie (plural) and du (singular) in German; vi (plural) and ti (singular) in Russian.

criminately, beyond finding each other's company amusing, beyond proximity. Friendship is very deep, and it includes emotional overtones and undertones.

In addition to being a matter of cultural differences, the differing interpretations of friendship also reflect the individual's personality, capacity for friendship, and experience. In every culture, some unfortunate people have no understanding of the word "friend" beyond the dictionary definition. They have never experienced a deep friendship, so they do not even know that it exists, and are therefore missing something in their lives. In some such cases, a dog may be the person's only "friend"—a rather limited friend, but at least it is a relationship in which both sides trust each other.

Other people know that deep friendship exists, but they cannot articulate it. It remains undefined, unclear, unused. The process of clarifying the meaning of friendship draws an outline, explores the boundaries of what exists, and creates the framework for developing the potential within the friendship. Real understanding, and a name for that understanding, creates the possibility for it to come into being. Without this process of recognizing, defining, and naming, if the friendship happens at all, it happens by chance. If so, it may not be appreciated until after it is gone, and the difference between "an acquaintance" and "a friend" realized only after the fact.

There is an Oriental Jewish romance from about 150 years ago that deals with the nature of this term. In this story, a father complains that his son spends too much money and time on his friends. The father inquires of the son how many friends he has, and the son estimates them to be about one hundred. The amazed father replies, "I have lived much longer than you, and in my entire life I have accumulated only one and a half friends."

They devise a plan to test the friends, whereby the son goes to one of his friends at midnight, carrying a loaded sack, saying that he has just killed the Crown Prince in a duel, and asking for help in burying the body and a place to hide. One friend after another throws him out immediately upon hearing the story, and none of them is willing to risk giving him help. The son returns to the father and says, "I understand now what you said about my friends, but are yours better?" The father then sends him first to his half-friend. The son knocks on the door at midnight, and upon hearing the story, the half-friend says, "You behaved very badly, but you are my friend's son, so come in. I will bury the body and hide you as best I can."

One of the things that emerge from this story is that one basic criterion of friendship is trust. Perhaps the utmost level of friendship, then, is trusting another person with your life. This type of friendship often develops in times of crisis, when people have to depend on each other for their lives, and especially in wartime. When people are comrades in arms, a tie of mutual interdependence and trust develops. Ancient Greek soldiers, for instance, would stand in rows, each holding a shield in his left hand and a sword in his right hand. They took an oath to fight, not to flee, and never to expose the person standing to their left. This mutual defense and dependability were essential to the integrity of the fighting unit.

Trust, which is crucial in a time of war, has to exist in ordinary, everyday life, too. Thus in business we have to trust the other party's honesty in order to be able to work together—we trust that the gasoline that we buy is indeed gasoline, and that the shirt we buy is made of what the label says. That, however, does not constitute friendship. It is possible to do business, or sign a political pact, with a person that we know is a crook; we just have to take measures to protect ourselves. In fact, it is sometimes easier to do business with a crook; because there is no trust, the parties will check each point of their agreement very carefully, and clarify the limits and boundaries of the "contract" they make, which—because there is no false trust —may be fulfilled in a satisfactory way. In any commercial deal or simple social exchange, the level of trust is limited.

Although doing business together does not necessarily imply friendship, business can also be defined and affected by friendship. It is important to know that there is at least one person whom one can lean on for a loan, one person who will not cheat. One of the main differences between business (commercial or social) and friendship is that business is basically an exchange of value for value, buying and selling. Friendship is an exchange of gifts, which should never be valued or measured. In fair commercial relationships, both sides are measured, the parties negotiate the worth, and they must always be equal, whereas in friendship, the exchange is not measured. The give-and-take of friendship may not be equal at all; one party may be the giver far more often than the other.

In fact, one of the tests of friendship is whether anyone is keeping accounts. Once a friend begins to keep accounts, even if the relationship continues in some form, it has become a commercial or semicommercial relationship, which is very different from a friendship. Thus, many supposed friendships (among them many boyfriend-girlfriend relationships) are actually commercial enterprises, in which one side gives the money, and the other side pays in behavior, influence, or some other currency. When one friend begins to calculate and compare what he gave and what he received, when one demands, or even thinks about, some return for his gifts—not only monetary value, but a kiss or a smile—the friendship has died and has become a business relationship.

Although the exchanges in friendship are not measured, friendship is mutual. Friends have to maintain a sense of equity. A parasite is not a friend. One party may be stronger, or the friends may rely on each other for different things, but there must be mutuality in the relationship; friends have to be able to lean on each other. The Bible says (Ecclesiastes 4:9–10), "Two are better than one, because they have a good return for their work. For if they fall, the one will lift up his fellow; but woe to him that is alone when he falls, for he has no one to help him up." This is not a deep psychological definition; it simply states the fact that a friend will lend a hand, will bail me out. Even if I never need that hand, a friend is someone I can lean on, who will not slip out from under me, leaving me off balance and alone. The Hebrew word for hand is *yad,* and one of the Hebrew words for friend is *yadid,* which is composed of *yad yad,* hand-hand,* giving each other a hand.

What, then, is the essence of friendship? It is the voluntary sharing with another of things that are important for me, whether it is sharing my possessions or my persona, my time or my secrets. In fact, this sharing does not always mean giving, but rather it is the will to allow somebody else to participate in something that is dear to me. Maimonides even goes so far as to say that the highest level of love is sharing the same objectives.[1] Indeed, some very intense friendships are based on sharing the same ideals, heroes, or even things of beauty.

As friendship intensifies, what deepens is the feeling of trust. The test of the depth and strength of the friendship might possibly be the level and depth of the trust between the friends. Can you trust the person with your possessions? With your feelings? With your life? Can you trust the person with deep secrets, or only with small secrets? If I can only trust my friend up to the sum of fifty thousand dollars, he may be a good business partner, but he is not a friend. If I trust my friend with money, then I have to be able to trust him with any amount of money. If I

*In Hebrew script, which is without vowels, the word is *ya-did, *while the word for "hand" is *yad.

trust that my friend will bail me out when I am in trouble, then I have to trust that my friend will bail me out of any kind of trouble, even if he disagrees with me, or thinks that I acted foolishly or viciously.

One may have a limited friendship, but the test of the true and real one is that it is not limited. Practically, people may have friendships that are confined to certain areas, friends in actual life and friends of the soul, friends that will share financial truths and friends that will share innermost thoughts. A complete friend is not limited, neither by the things shared nor by their magnitude. There is a Biblical verse that lists increasing degrees of intensity in relationships: "your brother, the son of your mother; or your son or daughter; or the wife of your bosom, or your friend who is as your own soul" (Deuteronomy 13:7). "Your friend who is as your own soul" is the ultimate friend, a real soul mate.

The Rebbe of Kotzk,* some 150 years ago, said that each person should have at least one friend that he can tell all his secrets to, even the most shameful ones. The secrets that one does not want to reveal are of two types: the first may be something that I am ashamed of, or simply something that I do not want publicized because, if revealed, it may cause me to be ridiculed or abused, it may be harmful to me financially or socially, or it may even be dangerous for me. The other kind of secret is a re-

Rabbi Menachem Mendel of Kotzk, one of the most outstanding Hassidic leaders.

serve, a shyness about revealing certain inner aspects of myself which I keep to myself, in myself. As a friendship intensifies, I gradually become ready to reveal more parts of myself.

People may be ashamed of their deeds or their thoughts; however, in most cases they are not embarrassed by them. It is not the misdeeds themselves but the fact that someone else knows about them that makes people blush. On the other hand, there are intimate emotions and ideas that are so private and so delicate, that exposing them is giving away the essence of their existence. In intense friendship, in which the other person feels as close as a second soul, everything can be revealed without embarrassment.

One of the primary distinctions between friendship and love is that friendship may be very intense and caring, but it does not lead to desire; it is love without desire. Friendships do sometimes develop into love affairs; but so long as they do not, friends can embrace each other or walk hand in hand without awakening desire, whereas love gradually intensifies, and its need for ever greater means of expression usually leads to physical involvement.*

Another major difference is that friendship is not exclusive. Most people cannot share lovers, but can share friends easily. A group of friends can include a range of in-

---

It is doubtful whether platonic love really exists, other than in books—mostly, not very good ones—and in Hollywood movies, where it is usually a cover-up for some other kind of relationship.

terrelationships that vary in closeness, intensity, and scope, without arousing jealousy. Friendship is also often exempt from the usual effects of time and distance. People can speak to each other only on rare occasions, or be separated from each other for years, yet be very close friends. This steadiness is a quality unique to friendship.

Even though a friendship may be an intense loving relationship, important and essential to one's life, it is also different and distinct from erotic love in that friendship, unlike love, does not seem to be blind. Love has a tendency to make people blind to the faults of the beloved. Friendship, in that sense, is broader-minded. I may see physical or personality blemishes in a friend; my friend may be insufferable, or a bore, or may have even worse qualities. Nevertheless, a friend is still a friend, and may be a close and very dear friend, even with a long list of blemishes. Moreover, even someone who is a liar will never lie to a friend, and one who is inept will do his best for a friend. Indeed, when choosing a friend we are not searching for a goddess or a knight on a white horse; rather, we are trying to find somebody we can rely on, with whom we can have a relationship that ties us together as a unit.

Friendship, like love, may develop in different forms. There may be "friendship at first sight," when people, who sometimes have seemingly very little in common, will immediately have a deep feeling of mutual affinity. In other cases, people may begin to define their relationship as a real friendship only after a lengthy process.

Like most precious things, friendship is hard to purchase. There is no currency, except friendship in return, that can pay for it. There are times when one identifies a person that one wants to befriend, but it may require a long time and much effort of "courting" to make the other person agree to accept the friendship. Making friends requires cultivating a relationship in a very sensitive way, because friendship, like love, is fragile. The hurt that results when the trust of friendship has been betrayed can be much deeper than the hurt of love betrayed.

Although a friendship seems far less emotional than a love affair, it is in many ways more sensitive. In fact, it seems that damaged friendship is harder to repair than damaged love, because love includes the element of desire, which somehow mends the fences. Because friendship does not have the glue of desire, friendship is like an egg: once it is broken, it is broken. When one discovers—even mistakenly—that one who is considered a friend cannot be trusted, then friendship can no longer exist. A lost friend can still be, for the other, a person to like or to admire, but broken trust breaks the very essence of friendship, and to rebuild it would require enormous effort.

This does not mean, however, that friends do not quarrel; friends can and do fight. In fact, one element of friendship is the permission to quarrel and still remain friends. However, not every friendship can withstand that. Friends usually know the limits of their friendship, and if problems arise, real friends can discuss them. A friendship that has to be defined in very clear terms, or one that has come to the point where the friends cannot talk anymore, has already fallen apart.

We are living in a time of unprecedented mobility and

ease of communication via any number of means. Most of us meet far more people than in the past, either in person or through other means. That does not mean that we create a greater number of deep relationships. On the contrary, a person in a crowd may feel as lonely as a person lost in a desert, possibly even lonelier. In our daily lives, just as in time of war or real struggle, there is a need for something to hang on to. That something is a stable, reliable relationship.

When we do not have that kind of relationship, and lack even the tools to create it, we hire professionals as substitutes for friends: we hire guards to protect us, and psychiatrists or lawyers to keep our secrets. But these are all commercial relationships. It is a very fortunate person who finds a person who is not just somebody to talk to, but a real friend. Friends do not have to be like each other. They may become like each other over time, but friendship is not based on similarity. The mutual feeling of compatibility transcends gender, race, language, and culture, as well as almost every other barrier.

Once we realize the importance of such a relationship, the word "friend" becomes far more loaded. We will use the term more cautiously, because it now has meaning and depth. Finding friendship is sometimes a matter of luck; sometimes, it requires prayer. If there is a lottery of life, then finding a genuine friend is a great prize.

Family

❧

Everybody is connected in one way or another with family. Besides being a part of the larger family—the family of man, or one's own people—everyone belongs to some sort of family.

People have diverse emotional responses to the notion of family, as well as to their own private families. For many people, even the word "family" has a strong appeal, because it evokes memories, the strongest of which is the feeling of deep love. There are people for whom the family connection is not only the most powerful tie they have, but the only relationship that really counts. They may easily change countries and nationalities, political and commercial affiliations, but they remain constant and loyal in their family ties. Others may be indifferent toward their families, viewing family simply as a fact of life that has to be accepted and dealt with in the best way possible. There are also people who actually dislike their families, or even hate them. Whatever the emotional relationship, families do exist, and everyone has to deal with them, both practically and emotionally.

It is usually accepted that the family is the basic unit of society. It may be enlarged and combined into bigger units: tribes, clans, peoples, or nations. The most modern large human unit, the nation, destroys other units, often intentionally, trying to break or at least to diminish the power of older groupings, such as tribes or clans. Yet even the most developed nations contain within themselves the smaller, ancient structure of the family. The family has remained the basic unit, not because it is the smallest, but because it is the most stable. It existed before any other human organization, and has remained with us throughout history. Because the notion of the family is so deeply implanted in us, differences of time and place may modify it, but they do not destroy it.

The fact that the family has continued to exist for such a long time does not mean that it is the most efficient of social structures. It is a rather inefficient unit when it comes to the labor force, economic resources, or the full development of individual capacity. Its stability and cohesiveness are apt to clash with national or religious aims. The inefficiency of the family as a working unit stems from its heterogeneity. With members of different sexes and ages, all in small numbers, the family cannot accomplish any task in a very fast and accurate way. The very successful groups of social insects (ants, bees, termites) are composed mostly of neuters—the workers and the soldiers of the lot. They prove the efficiency of a family-less, homogeneous worker society.

Families also have their special interests, and they tend to develop them, even at the expense of larger outside social units. For instance: the desire to grant children (through inheritance) a share of money or power creates inequality and results in some inept people having more influence than they merit.

Even for breeding purposes, the family is not very efficient. Biologically speaking, families have the advantage of maintaining a very diverse gene pool. However, they also create a large number of people who are affected by genetic anomalies, and even the very process of having children and raising them within the family is obviously not always successful.

The emotional and practical ties within the family also hamper individual growth. Taking care of children, providing for them, having to pay attention to the spouse, keeping some kind of a household—all these may be emotionally satisfying, but they also consume enormous amounts of time and energy. It is very difficult to be a great writer or an ecstatic worshipper, or to breed tarantulas, when the family does not agree with these occupations.

These are the reasons why so many societies have tried to disrupt, or at least weaken, the power of the family.

Some societies tried to maintain a population of individuals without families. Slavery was not only a way of creating cheap labor. It was also a deliberate method for breaking up family units, and developing a more efficient labor force. In the Middle Ages, there were even remarkable—and successful—slave armies, like the Mamelukes in Egypt.

The extensive use of eunuchs was another way of producing people without family ties. Beyond being used as harem keepers, they also served as soldiers and generals, and even held important political positions.* In a different way, monastic orders and celibate priesthoods—in many countries, from the West to the Far East—were also strategies for creating elite groups without family units. The Janissaries, who formed the elite of the rising Ottoman empire, were both slaves and celibate. Relaxing the laws of celibacy turned out to have been one of the factors that contributed to their decline. Throughout the ages, totalitarian regimes have also attempted to break the family unit of their slaves, their subject nations, and even their own people.[1]

It is far more difficult to manipulate and maneuver

---

*For example, the Byzantine general Narses (480–574); or the tradition of having eunuchs in high position, which existed in China for a very long time, from antiquity to the end of the Chinese empire in the twentieth century. Rule by eunuchs was also the practice in certain periods in both ancient Persia and Rome.

families than it is to deal with family-less individuals. To achieve certain objectives, one has to destroy this unit. Sometimes, the urge to destroy, or flee, the family comes from within. In many contemporary societies, the disruption of the family is caused mainly by the individual's growing desire for the unhampered pursuit of self.

Despite all the attempts made throughout history to destroy the family, this ancient unit—precisely because it is so primitive and so deeply embedded within us—eventually regains its place. It is such a basic unit that it is not exclusively human; families also exist among many other creatures in the world. Moreover, they exist not only in highly developed life-forms, but among relatively primitive creatures, such as birds.

The fact that family is not a uniquely human phenomenon demonstrates that it is not just a concept, an artificial social construct, but a part of nature itself. It may be irrational and inefficient, troublesome and inconvenient, but it endures, because it goes deeper than reason. Although numbing the instincts may break their compulsion, instincts never disappear completely. Individuals—even a large number of them, if the culture and spirit of the times allow for it—can live without family ties; but the human spirit as a whole will stick to them. Cultural fashions are essentially ephemeral; instincts are not.

Family seems to begin with a very simple need—a sexual connection. Sexual attraction is a very strong biological drive that we certainly know exists, even though we do not fully understand it. However, in itself, attraction does not necessarily create family. It certainly moves one toward fulfilling its aim—copulation—but whether it lasts for a minute or for a longer period, this connection ceases once the desire is fulfilled. Such single-purpose relations do not form families, neither in the animal world (as with most fish and reptiles), nor among humans.

A family structure begins when parents remain connected to each other in order to raise their offspring. This urge to have a family is an instinct, a very distinct drive that has little to do with sex. The male bird searching for food for the female and fledglings, or the lioness hunting food for her cubs, are not motivated by sex.* In many cases, the family tie is temporary; it endures only long enough to enable the offspring to survive independently. These units form and re-form according to chance or selection, but have no continuity. Moreover, not all families, animal or human, are monogamous. The titmouse birds, for example, usually live, and even migrate, in one-sex groups, forming temporary "families" in the breeding seasons. Such behavior is not confined to this species alone, but is found among a number of other species as well, including humans.

It seems, then, that even for animals, and most certainly for humans, sex and procreation are not the sole el-

---

The fact that the neuter workers among the social insects also take care of, and feed, their siblings is conclusive proof that this drive to take care of the young has nothing to do with the sexual desire.

ements that create a family. Propagation of the species is surely an important need, and offspring may be a central part of the family structure, but they are not what define it. Both sex and procreation can, and do, exist independently, outside of the family. The family is, therefore, something that contains these elements, but goes beyond them.

The element of permanence, which remains even when the partners are no longer occupied with sex or with raising offspring, is one mark of the family. Such permanent families exist not only among humans; there are some animals and birds that have strong family connections for many years, sometimes (among swans and geese, for example) even for a lifetime.

Among some social birds (such as jackdaws), we can find some striking examples of behaviors that we consider "human": they form permanent couples, their social position (or pecking order) changes upon their "marriage," and they even have an "engagement" period—a certain amount of time prior to the sexual activity, in which they spend time together and are considered a couple by the other members of the group. Even details of the family structure, which are deemed to be only social conventions, are actually very deeply embedded in a general biological format. In addition, members of a family unit—whether it is a couple, parent(s) and offspring, siblings, or more extended relatives—provide each other with mutual support and protection above and beyond the norm prevailing in the group to which they belong.

All of this, however, is an outside, biological, or sociological view of the family. What is the inner, mental-
emotional aspect that defines and creates it?

We have many images of family, some of them highly
sentimental. The most common romantic notion is that
the family is a place of shared love. It may indeed be true
that in many cases all the members of the family do enjoy
each other's company, and like and even love each other,
but obviously, kinship is not always synonymous with
love. The feeling that "blood is thicker than water" may
be strong and compelling, even when there is very little
love involved. For many people there are other, far more
powerful objects of love outside of the family: friends,
comrades in a group, co-religionists, and the like. Usually,
erotic love is far more intense than familial love, even
though not as enduring.

Not infrequently, members of a family rather dislike
each other. Freud says, "If there is a person that a woman
dislikes more than her sister, it is possibly her mother."[2]
Although this may not be a universal feeling, it is common enough to deserve notice; it shows that family structure, and even bonds of close kinship, are not based
exclusively on love.

Even though family is not always a place of mutual
love, closeness and togetherness are some other distinctive marks. This togetherness has a twofold source. Su-
perficially, it seems to be the result of being in close
physical proximity over a long period of time. However,
extreme closeness is no guarantee of affection—some-

times, quite the opposite; yet it does ensure the creation of a special relationship.* Knowing someone from infancy (mine, or the other person's) creates a distinct bond, strengthened by the awareness that this bond will never break.

There is another, more internal reason for closeness: members of the same family are genetically—and therefore, also physically and mentally—similar to each other. This similarity, in itself, creates a bond of deeper mutual understanding.† Such understanding does not always develop into mutual love, because of the resentment we may feel toward members of our family, which is often the result of self-criticism, sometimes conscious, but more often unconscious. Many people who are harshly critical of, say, their fathers come to realize how similar they are to them, and how they share those faults that they resent so much in their parents. This twofold closeness is very much an inner, emotional part of family.

Yet with all these internal and external traits, what the defining characteristic of family is based on is a contract. Again, this is true of both human and animal families. A

This can be observed, for instance, when one finds a relative—even a very close one—with whom one was not in contact, for whatever reason. The relationship, which legally may be a very close one, is not so emotionally.

†*Twins, especially identical ones, are well-known examples of this kind of very close connection, even when they are not raised in the same place.*

well-defined relationship exists among family members, which marks their obligations to each other, and it is this mutual obligation that forms the family. When there is no obligation, there may be a love affair, or a breeding plant—but not a family. This may seem like a very cold, remote, legalistic, and technical definition of family, but it is realistic and accurate, and this mutual obligation forms the stable basis of the family.

"Contract" is, of course, a human term; it does not apply to animals. Even among humans, who are able to form contracts, most such agreements are never written, or even expressed explicitly. Surely, a family formed by two birds or two monkeys is based on nonverbal understandings, basic agreements for mutual interaction, which they nevertheless keep. On the other hand, even an old-fashioned, written contractual husband-wife relationship may change enormously over time—not only in the course of generations, but even within the life span of the same family. Yet, as long as it is a mutual agreement that both sides accept and keep, the family remains a family. All the rest is additional, optional, and not entirely necessary for building and maintaining the basic family structure.

Whatever the family's agreement may be, it is always based on mutual trust. No family can exist if one of its members is mortally afraid of being harmed by another member. There are no spider families because female spiders try to devour the males. On the other hand, two wolves living together are ferocious animals that can harm each other considerably. The fact that they are a pair means that they have an agreement not to do so, as well as a pact to fight for those things that are for their mutual good—because mutual protection is also part of the family contract. Thus, without signing any legal papers, when the female bird is hatching the eggs, the male bird feeds it, and in that relationship both partners perform their share of the agreement.

As an example: an integral part of the Jewish marriage ceremony is the reading aloud of the *Ketubah* (a written summary of some of the marital obligations). The existence of such a contract is what makes the difference between marriage and prostitution, between a family relationship and a love affair. Although there are standard forms of this contract (which is primarily a list of the husband's obligations toward the wife), there may still be quite a diversity in form and content.* What matters is that it is a long-term contract which both parties accept. The prophet Hosea (3:3) expressed this kind of relationship concisely: "And I said to her, you shall abide for me many days, you shall not play the harlot, and you shall not be for another man, so will I also be for you."

For example, one Jewish source—Tosefta, Ketubot 4:7—tells about the son of the great sage Rabbi Akiva, who took his wife to court in order to settle some financial matters. He told the court, "I am not fighting anything here; it would be best to let her speak up and tell you the facts." From the wife's testimony it was discovered that their marriage contract said that he would take her as his wife on condition that she feed him, clothe him, and teach him Torah. This is a rather unusual marriage contract indeed, but it is nevertheless a valid contract.

This essential element of family relations exists not only between spouses, but also between parents and children and among siblings. What makes them into a family is not the fact that they love each other, or that those parents begot those particular children, but that they understand and keep their obligations toward each other.

Remember that the Ten Commandments do not say, "Love your father and mother." Parents may want love very much; some of them may demand it, and even make the lives of the children miserable if they think that they do not get enough of it. However, love is neither commanded nor demanded; rather, the commandment is (Exodus 20:12), "Honor your father and your mother." Love within the family is a very good thing, but the commandment is to honor—or, in other words, to keep the formal and informal obligations of children toward parents. That is true about siblings as well. Far beyond the love or the biological connection, it is the mutual obligation between them that comprises the core family tie.

I want to stress this point, because we are living in a time, and within a culture, that often substitutes love for obligation. Through the influence of romantic literature, among other reasons, we tend to think that love makes the family. Love may make the family a glorious place to be, but it is keeping the rules—whatever these may be, and they do change from one culture to another, and from one family to another—that creates the family.

Family that is based on a foundation of emotion, however strong and durable that emotion may be, is actually built on fiction. Romantic love may be an enormous drive; people think and dream about it, sometimes even die for it. However, a great part of that romantic love is based on cultural clichés and ephemeral chemical reactions. A love that is triggered, and sometimes sustained, by a certain turn of the nose or a pair of beautiful legs is not real enough to endure. La Rochefoucauld wrote that had it not been for romantic novels, many people would never fall in love.

When people base their families on love alone, that family relationship reflects a fictionalized picture of each other and of the mutual relationship. In the fortunate cases, romantic love is replaced by a more enduring (though less glamorous) love for the other person, which also includes the difficult elements of accepting the other person's faults, and taking on obligations. However, when such love does not develop, the family remains a piece of fiction that will not last. A family that was built from the outset on fictitious ideas will not withstand financial, emotional, or social stress, or the spouses will imagine that they love others, outside the family.

As this kind of fiction gains influence in a society, the family unit becomes increasingly unstable. The dream evaporates fast enough, to be replaced either by another, equally fictitious affair, or by sheer indifference. Inertia, or various practical considerations, may prolong the tie for some time, but the problems and stresses that invariably crop up in life will eventually topple it. We can see evidence of this in the United States, all over Europe, and

in Russia, where families tend to collapse under any kind
of pressure.

This burden of obligation does not mean that people
have to suffer continuously within the family. On the contrary, family can be fun. It may be thoroughly delightful
to be with one's family members; one may derive joy and
happiness from them, and there may even be a glow of
love all around. Yet that happy state is, invariably, an outcome of getting first things first, of doing things in the
right order. This basic element of mutual obligation is the
soil in which all other things—love, emotional support,
and fun—can grow, never the other way around. The
stronger the understanding that the family is bound by
rules and agreements, the more permanent it will be.

In any social unit—and the family is no exception—
members may have disagreements about many things,
most things, or even everything. Nevertheless, as long as
they stick to the basic rules of the relationship, that unit
will survive. Being within a family in whatever role, as
child or parent, sibling or spouse, does not preclude the
ability or the desire—sometimes the huge temptation—to
have a nice big fight. Although fighting is not one of the
musts of family, it seems that family members do feel that
having a good fight from time to time is just as necessary
as being in love, if not more so.

These fights are often like ritualized duels: you try to
stab me, I try to stab you; you say bad things about me, I
say bad things about you. However, both parties know
that there is no killing involved. A family fight may be-

come ferocious, but underlying it is the understanding and the knowledge that the basic agreement still exists. In a way, it is a test of the agreement. It may not always be done playfully; sometimes it is done in deadly earnestness, and all the parties involved may feel deeply hurt. However, it will not break up the relationship. Siblings will fight with each other, if they can, almost without exception, but it is as if they were saying, "I am entitled to beat up my brother, and he truly deserves it, but I will protect him with my life against anybody else."

When a unit is stable, whatever fights occur in it are contained within its structure. Once that structure is weakened, a fight usually means the end of the relationship and the dismantling of the unit. In families that are based on fiction, when there is disagreement, family members no longer say, "We disagree, but we are still a family." Instead they say, "We disagree, and therefore we can no longer be together."

There is a lot of talk nowadays about "family values," but what are they? They are simply those very basic agreements that govern personal and interpersonal behavior. In essence, they are the same values that make any kind of society work. All social units are based on some kind of agreement, either tacit or explicit. Agreement makes society function, from its largest constructs down to its most basic unit, the family.

This understanding of family is both more, and less, than what people expect: less, because it includes no sentimental gushing; more, because it takes family far too seriously to let it pass as a play that people take up with each other for a shorter or longer time. Family is, in fact, the outcome and expression of a law, albeit not necessarily a written one. It is not a religious or moral dictum, since animals, too, have it.

Family, then, is a deep connection that goes beyond a whimsical feeling, beyond an urge, beyond emotional up-heaval. Members of a family are bound by obligation, con-nected to each other by the knowledge that they can rely on each other. Only such inviolable contractual obligation can serve as a stable basis for family.

Love

⊸

T h e word "love" is used in a multitude of contexts, with a myriad of connotations, embracing a wide range of emotions, from the most trivial whim to the most sublime philosophical idea. We all think we know what love means, but precisely because the word is used so often, and in so many ways, it has become fuzzy, obscure, even meaningless. Love of God, love of one's country, love of a spouse, love of children, and love of herring may all be called "love," but they are clearly not the same feeling. Even the expression "making love" refers to an act that does not necessarily have anything to do with love, or, for that matter, any other emotion.

The word "love" is used and misused in so many ways. It refers to emotions that range from the very low to the very high, and may differ considerably in intensity: from a rather weak inclination to an overwhelming passion. Therefore, it is necessary to begin our discussion with the simplest and broadest definition.

The very first element in any kind of love is caring about something. There cannot be love when one does not care. The real opposite of love is not hate, but indifference. The emotions of love and hate do indeed pull in opposite directions; while love means being drawn toward the object of our emotions, hatred is pulling away from it. Yet both love and hate begin with caring. The emotion may not be constant; it may vacillate between love and hate, but the core feeling is, fundamentally, one of caring, of being involved. Only when one is involved can an emotion—positive or negative—develop. It therefore happens that people have ambivalent feelings of love and hate mingled together.

In many cases, the emotional involvement may reverse: passionate love may sometimes turn into passionate hate, as happens in cases of disappointment in love. Jealousy is another common case of deep love that has turned into fierce hatred. As the verse in the Song of Songs (8:6) puts it, "Love is strong as death, jealousy is cruel as the grave." It may happen in the opposite direction as well, with hatred turning into love. In any case, the emotion depends on caring about something. On the other hand, when one no longer cares, the object becomes insignificant, and is neither loved nor hated, Indifference is the death of any emotional bond.

Caring is the foundation of love, but it is not the emotion itself. Caring about anything may develop in directions other than love. It may turn into respect or admiration, as happens sometimes when one deals with important people or significant subjects. Thus, one may respect the science of biophysics, or admire a great philosopher. This results in a certain emotional response, but that response will not be love. On the other hand, one may care about something that is dangerous or harmful: an abyss alongside a road, or a tiger on the way. There will be an emotional response—fear, and an attempt to avoid the danger—but it will not be hatred.

Love begins when this caring is not only an objective appraisal, but becomes a personal attachment, when the object is not just "a thing" or "a person" that is judged by itself, but when one becomes involved in the relationship. Certain physical attributes, as well as some mental and emotional responses, are found among people everywhere. A certain amount of caring seems to be inherent in our existence. Love, however, seems to be on a different plane; it seems that love is something that people have to learn. As children develop, first they know and care only about themselves, because they do not really have a clear notion of "outside." As they grow, they begin to find the other, first as a reflection of their own image, then as a separate entity. When they see a creature that is different from themselves, yet somewhat similar, they begin to have a relationship; they begin to care for the other.

The capacity for love may be inborn, but it does not always develop. It may take time and experience until it happens. Caring may develop into compassion—which literally means to feel passion together with another. When compassion grows, the emotional involvement deepens, and then becomes the emotion of love.

Love, then, is the emotion of attraction toward an object—the beloved. But this feeling of attraction is not a single, well-defined emotion. Because of the great variety in personalities, the differences in the object of love, and the vagueness of the term, there may be many different relationships that people will call "love."

There is a Jewish folk tale that illustrates how vague the meaning of the word "love" can be, and also it demonstrates some of the basic problems in statements such as "I love you." Once upon a time, a fisherman caught a large pike, and when he pulled the fish out of the water and saw its size, he said, "This is wonderful! I'll take it to the Baron; he loves pike." The poor fish says to himself, "There's some hope for me yet." The fisherman brings the fish to the manor house, and the guard says, "What do you have?" "A pike." "Great," says the guard. "The Baron loves pike." The fish feels that there is some corroboration of the facts. The fisherman enters the palace, and though the fish can hardly breathe, he still has hope: the Baron loves pike. He is brought into the kitchen, and all the cooks exclaim how much the Baron loves pike. The fish is placed on a table, and the Baron himself enters, and gives instructions, "Cut off the tail, cut off the head, and slit it this way." With his last breath, the fish cries out in great despair, "Why did you lie? You don't love pike, you love yourself!"

The poor fish clearly had a linguistic-philological problem. It confused two different meanings of the same verb. This raises the question: are these two meanings really so different from each other? Don't people make the same mistake when they think and talk about love? There is "fish love," and there is Love. Clearly, they are not the same. They do not have the same emotional impact, and what is more important, the emotions themselves are not the same.

The various kinds of love differ both in quantity— namely, in how strong and compelling the emotion is— and, more significantly, in quality. Different loves are distinguished from one another by the object of love, and by the feeling itself. Usually, people instinctively differentiate between the different kinds of love, but when they do mix them up, it may become ridiculous, bizarre, and even perverse. A person who is in love will frequently form an attachment to objects that belong to the beloved as well. However, when the emotion toward the beloved's shoe becomes identical to the emotion toward the person, there is a clear case of perversion (fetishism, to use the clinical term). If one loves children in the same way one loves a spouse (or vice versa), this, too, is obviously a mental illness.

With all the emotional differences among the various "loves," they have many things in common. In every love there is strong positive feeling and deep attraction to the beloved, whether it is a person, an idea, or an inanimate object. What "fish love" and Love have in common—in fact, what every form of love has, from the most exalted to the most prosaic—are three components: the subject (the lover), an emotion (love), and an object (the beloved). The nature of the love depends on each of them alone, and on the interrelationships among them.

The most exalted kind of love is something that most people can speak about only theoretically. Poets and philosophers write about it, people in love speak about it, and many others yearn for it, but most of us have never experienced it. It is a love that is entirely object-oriented; the lover does not care what benefit or enjoyment he gains from the beloved. The emotional drive, as well as the joy of that love, is in the feeling of love itself. I love something, and I love it as it is, just because it is. I do not need to possess it, or even to have a response from my beloved. Sometimes, the only wish of the lover is just to be as close as possible to the beloved. In higher forms, even this desire does not occur, because the love is just the joy that the beloved exists, and that is enough.

One example of this love may be admiring a beautiful mountain. I do not care whether the mountain responds, whether the mountain loves me back. I also do not want to take it with me. I leave it as it is. I can admire it, I can even experience an intense feeling of love, but I have no desire to possess it, nor do I expect it to give me anything in return.

In most cases, however, love is not so "detached." If I

love flowers, and I find a beautiful flower, how should I best express that feeling: by picking it, or by letting it be? If I really love the flower in itself and for itself, the beauty of it, the smell of it, then I should leave it as it is. That would be object-oriented love. However, most people would pick the flower, which means that they not only want to love it, but also to possess it. They are willing to destroy the flower in order to enjoy it. That is also love, but of another kind; it is clearly a subject-oriented love.

The difference between object-oriented and subject-oriented love can be very subtle. Complicating the issue is the fact that anything is liable to become "misused" as the subject of subject-oriented love. In the fish story, it is clear that the Baron's love of pike is completely selfish, and that he cares nothing for the fish, its welfare or its life. He just likes (or even passionately loves) the taste of the fish, because he loves himself, and one of his ways of satisfying that love is by eating the fish. When it comes to human relationships that are more complex, it is not always that clear. Whatever the object of love may be, the question is always: what do I love? Do I really love the object, or do I love myself, and just want to gratify my desires by means of the object?

This problem is very well recognized in the realm of erotic or sensual love. Does one really love the beloved as a person, or is the love only a pretext to have sex with another, enjoying oneself by means of the other, a true "fish love"? There are far more subtle cases. For instance, some people say they love their children, but in truth, they use the youngsters for their own enjoyment. This enjoyment may not necessarily be physical; perhaps they like meddling with another person's life, or having somebody to pet. Either way, it is themselves they care for, not the children. If I need an object, and I keep it in order to meet my needs, I am not really interested in the object, I am just interested in its usefulness to me. Whether the enjoyment is spiritual or material, whether it is simply possessiveness, or gross physical abuse for the sake of enjoyment—if it is about what the object provides for the subject, it is not ideal, selfless love.

This way of probing into the nature of love may become very disturbing. Self-interest may persist from the grossest material benefit to very refined and spiritual forms. One should ask, "How much of my love is simply self-gratification?" It is possible for love of God to be the same as love of pike, e.g., when religiosity is based on one's needs for security, as a crutch for a failing individual, or mostly when it is centered on "what will I get from it."

In every "I love you," whoever or whatever the love and the "you" are, there is always an "I." A self must always be involved in the process; the emotion of love cannot exist without a self. Even when love requires great self-denial, it still requires a self at the center of the emotion. It is impossible for love to be entirely devoid of self, because somebody has to be the carrier, the feeler of the emotion.

Indeed, the quality of the emotion of love, the feeling,

depends as much upon the subject, the personality of the lover, as upon the object. Some personalities are fiery: their emotion has to rise to higher and higher levels. Others do not have any need for storms; they even prefer a quiet life. Indeed, Jewish sources describe these two kinds of loves as "love like fire" and "love like water."[1] "Love like fire" consumes, it burns a person, while "love like water" is satisfying, soothing.

At first glance, it may seem that the "love like fire" is desire, and "love like water" is fulfillment, but that is not necessarily so; there is a difference in the nature of the emotion itself. A lover consumed with "love like fire" may burn with a compelling need to do something about that love; it makes the lover less and less happy—consumed, but not happy, not joyful. To express their love, some have to shower the beloved with gifts—not in order to bribe or possess the beloved, but as an expression of their burning desire. Yet the more they express it, the more the desire grows. In a sense, those gifts have less to do with the recipient than with the giver: the giver has the satisfaction of giving, of expressing love.* Martyrdom is the ultimate expression of love that cannot be satisfied until it is sacrificial, because it is an all-consuming feeling. In contrast, in "love like water," the very existence of the beloved is enough to make the lover happy.

*Indeed, one of the differences between giving charity and giving out of love is that charity is object-oriented; it is connected, or should be connected, with the needs of the recipient.

Just as the personality of the lover affects the nature of the love, the object of the love is also essential to the relationship. Not all beloveds lend themselves to the same kind of love; some objects, almost by their very nature, can only be loved in one form and not in another. Loving a beautiful thing and loving food are not the same kind of love; the beautiful object and the food are utilized in different ways.

Some people are so in love with money that they have an almost physical craving for it. The miser who will not use his money derives immense satisfaction just from knowing that he has it. In that case, the money becomes an abstract ideal. One might say that the miser's love is a very delicate kind of love; he does not need anything from his beloved, he does not use his beloved; he is just happy that it is there for him. I once heard about a miserly old man who had a young girl living with him. Everybody told him that it was not he she loved, but his money. To this the miser retorted, "I spent my whole life making money, thinking about money; that was the only thing that really interested me. What am I? I am my money. If she loves the money, she loves me dearly." He identified so with his money that it was no longer just something that he possessed; it was his very self.

The sages of the Talmud differentiate between conditional and unconditional love.[2] In conditional love, fulfillment often results in the end of love. Amnon, the son of King David, fell madly in love with his half-sister Tamar. He tricked her into coming to his bedroom, and despite her pleas, he raped her. "Afterward, Amnon hated her with an intense hatred; he hated her with a hatred even greater than his former love," and he threw her out of his house. This example—a particular historical instance of something that happens frequently—shows how people may deceive even themselves by confusing emotions. Amnon thought that he loved the girl, while in truth he just had a very intense sexual desire. He really wanted something very concrete, and once he got it, Tamar became like a used rag for him: ugly, dirty, and not worth keeping.[3]

Amnon's "love" was clearly conditional. In other cases, however, differentiating between love for a quality or attribute of the beloved, and a higher, more refined love for the person or object, may be a far more delicate matter. If I love someone because he or she is beautiful, clever, powerful, or has some other quality, is it the person that I care about, or is it the quality? Does love connect to an essential self in the beloved, or just to a list of attributes? The question goes even further than that: does love require attributes in the beloved in order to exist? Is love rational, at least in the sense that it increases as the attributes get better, more beautiful, more bountiful, more anything? Or is love blind?

It seems that there does not have to be any real connection between the emotion of love and the object of love. Consider the most common kind of love: self-love. Of course, this love is usually quite different from falling in love with another person. Except for pathological cases (extreme narcissism), it does not include any fiery emotion. Still, it has all the elements of love: the attachment, the involvement, the desire to grant the beloved (oneself, that is) every whim, and so on. Because we are born with it, there is no strong emotional display, very much like love within the family; yet it is a very stable and enduring love.

Self-love provides powerful evidence of two important, broadly applicable aspects of love. First, love is blind—or, better yet, hallucinatory. Most people love themselves even though they know more derogatory things about themselves than anybody else could ever find out. In most cases, self-love is a full-fledged, everlasting love affair, and, although it sometimes grows and sometimes diminishes, it exists independently of any special attributes.

Similarly, when I adore a person, a thing, a picture, or an abstract notion, I may be mistaken; I may be blinded by emotion, prejudice, or a chemical reaction. Nevertheless, as long as the imaginary quality exists for me, as long as I see it, the feeling lasts. The imaginary beauty is beautiful, as long as I imagine it to be so. People who fall in love become blind; they do not see the crooked nose or the terrible mental qualities of the beloved. In this case, beauty is indeed in the eye of the beholder. To the male warthog, the female warthog possesses every kind of beauty. It is only when the illusion stops that one realizes there was no substance there, that one loved an illusion, without valid grounds to base it on.

The second aspect of love epitomized by self-love is forgiveness. Even people who are not forgiving—by religion or by temperament—are ready to forgive themselves, and forget almost everything. Forgiveness does not mean that people ignore all their own flaws, but they are able to go on loving themselves, even with all the faults and all the guilt. How does this happen? At a certain point, when people begin to develop a sense of self, they fall in love with this self, and they cease to demand anything of it; its mere existence is enough for them. Love rarely distorts facts; it covers up faults by changing our estimation of them. Facts somehow do not sound the same, or matter quite as much, when they are about me.

When I love someone, whether it is my child, my spouse, or any other person, I may see the whole person, including the faults, but I just do not care about these faults. In a sense, it is like looking at an airplane propeller. As long as it is moving very fast, one cannot see the blades; once one begins to see them, it means that the propeller is no longer functioning. As long as one looks at the object of love and sees no flaws—just, perhaps, a little blur—then everything is all right. When one begins to focus on details, the appreciation of the whole person is lost, and the love can no longer override the flaws.

A loftier instance of love, however, is described in the Book of Genesis (29:20): "Jacob worked to get Rachel for seven years, and they were like several days in his eyes, because of his love for her." At first glance, that seems paradoxical—not just because seven years is a long time, but because when one in love is separated from the beloved, a day seems like a year. Yet here, it says just the opposite: seven years was like several days.

If the love of the other is for one's own satisfaction, then being separated from the object of love causes suffering; the more intense the feeling, the longer, subjectively, time seems. When I truly love the other just because the beloved exists, not because I want anything, then seven years and three days are exactly the same. What I really get from the love is the love itself. What matters is the relationship, not the benefits derived from it. My beloved exists, and therefore all is well; I need nothing more, not a smile or a look in return for my love. I do not even need my beloved to notice me. Theoretically, the greater the love, the more it is centered on the object and the less it has to do with the subject. Ideal love is concentrated on the beloved and nowhere else; the lover feels love, and does not require anything in return.

The loftiest kind of love, the love of God, is described in the Book of Job (13:15). It says there: "Even when He kills me, I still yearn for Him." When I am aware that You, God, are there, everything is all right—not because the world is perfect, or all is well with my life, or because this makes me richer or happier. Life is all right because You exist, and that in itself provides all the satisfaction I need. Job's extreme statement defines the most unconditional kind of love.

Some people are born with a great gift for love, while others have to learn love from the very basics—possibly by expanding self-love into love for others. For others yet, love is a very difficult exercise, and in order to achieve it, even to the smallest degree, they have to make deep structural personality changes. Some people experience love only for a fleeting moment. Only a few—possibly, those who have this gift from birth—are willing, and able, to attain totally unconditional love.

God

⌇

Many of us will honestly say, "I would like to believe in God. If only I could see something, anything, that proves that God exists, I would gladly accept and believe." Unfortunately, what most people can see of God would be irrelevant or nonsensical, and what is relevant and sensible cannot be seen.

There is a Yiddish folk song that deals with that very problem in a way that is both frivolous and profound:

> The skeptic asks the believer,
> "What is God? What is God?"
> Says the believer to the skeptic,
> "You donkey, you donkey you,
> There is no thought that can grasp Him,
> There is no place that is not filled with Him."[1]

The skeptic asks the believer,
"Where is God? Where is God?"
Says the believer to the skeptic,
"There is no place that is not filled with Him,
There is no thought that can encompass Him."

This little ditty seems to bring the problem of belief in God to an impasse. For those who already believe, the questions are irrelevant. For those who are outside the realm of belief, it is the answers that are irrelevant. However, there is a different question that is relevant for both believer and nonbeliever alike: what is it that you do or do not believe in? This is not an issue of high theology. It is a very close, concrete matter that affects people in every station of life, whether they are intellectual and sophisticated, or simple, emotional types.

Perhaps our greatest difficulty in relating to God is our inherent inability to form any coherent understanding of the Almighty. With the millions of words that have been said and written, both for and against, with all the prayers, prayer books, and books on devotion, so much of this subject still remains empty words. The word "God" is indeed used—in public prayers or in unvoiced wishes, in common conversation and in curses—with equal meaninglessness. For most people, it means everything—and nothing.

The source of this confusion is, of course, the subject itself. We make it worse, since we use the word "God" without thinking about it. We trust all kinds of constructs that should be helpful crutches, but these crutches may actually cripple us instead.

One of the most common crutches we use is anthropomorphism. It is very hard to have an emotional relationship with something that is entirely different, so we use anthropomorphic images to help us. Basically, we can only relate to what we see in the mirror. We depict everything in our own image. How do we understand others? We extrapolate from ourselves. Rightly or wrongly, that is the only way we can understand the other. In order to understand the world emotionally, we anthropomorphize— we elevate the low, and we lower the high.[2] We do it with animals, we do it with trees, and we do it with inanimate objects, because that is how we can relate emotionally.

For instance, we speak about the foot of a mountain; we know that a mountain does not have feet, but giving it a human image helps to create an emotional appeal. If we have a cat, we do the same thing—we make the cat into a human being. Even aliens and robots in science fiction films are given human attributes to enable us to relate to them. It would be much harder to relate to an alien that looked like an amoeba. Manufacturers now give human voices to computers and cars. Why? There is no intrinsic need, but we become emotionally attached to objects with human characteristics. This is not rational, it may even be one of our human limitations—but the need to anthropomorphize is deep within us.

When we need an emotional relationship, we create images; that is why poetry is full of images. The more images we create, the more emotions we can have. Just imagine a love letter written by a mathematician, describing his beloved's eyes as ellipsoids. It may be mathematically accurate, but it will not arouse much emotion—neither in the giver nor in the receiver. We need the images; they are part of our emotional heritage, but they are limited, by definition. Poetry is wonderful, but we should not expect God to conform to our images.

Yet we do. For many people, the image of God is quite clear: a big, white-bearded man sitting on a throne very high in the sky. He has—at least figuratively—a stick in one hand, and a bag of candy in the other, bestowing each on His subjects. Many prayers, as well as bitter complaints, ask for more of the candy and less of the stick. You may object and say that such an idea is just childish, kindergarten imagery, but how many people actually continue to develop their religious understanding beyond that age?

As enticing as this grandfather image of God is, it contains within itself its own destruction. The budding atheist or agnostic eleven- or twelve-year-old is one who cannot—with full justification—continue believing in this definition of God. Unfortunately, most adolescents throw away the whole idea of God along with this picture. Because they do not have the ability, or desire, to transform this childish description, they remain atheists or agnostics for the rest of their lives. Years ago, when the first Soviet cosmonauts returned from space, Khrushchev asked them, "Did you see anybody up there?" When they told him they did not see anyone, Khrushchev gleefully pronounced that to be the final proof that God does not exist.

More sophisticated people, who do not expect to see the Almighty walking around in a long white robe, ask for miracles as proof of God's existence. If God does not appear in person, at least He should appear in a miracle. If God wants to prove His existence without showing His face, perhaps He could do something obvious and spectacular. Philosophically, however—as pointed out many years ago by Maimonides[3]—a miracle does not really prove anything. A miracle merely proves that something extraordinary happened, and no more. A miracle that goes against what we call the laws of nature is simply what it is: something astonishing. It does not have an intrinsic message. Turning a glass of wine into a flower is remarkable, astonishing, and spectacular, but it does not prove that two times two equals five and a half, nor that God exists. One thing has nothing to do with the other. The sea being split or a pillar of fire has nothing to do with anything beyond what they are.

This observation about the invalidity of miracles as proof of God's existence was used at the time when science was far more rigid. In our time, it is much less effective. What is the difference between a nineteenth-century scientist and a twentieth-century scientist? If a devil appeared to a nineteenth-century scientist, he would say, "You do not exist." The twentieth-century scientist would look at him and say, "You are a phenomenon." The scientist just writes down that he saw a phenomenon of smaller or bigger magnitude. However, even this change in the way science views things makes no difference as far as faith is concerned. Even if people today accept a concept like "miracle" and do not ignore it, or fight against it, this does not necessarily change their worldview. Namely, they may see a miracle, note it, and then go on with their lives, without its having any effect on other spheres of their lives. In other words, although science has changed, it has not altered its basic attitude toward miracles.

Since early times, many people have deplored the fact that we no longer see miracles, while others just wonder why we do not have miracles. Perhaps miracles do still happen, but we do not observe them. When we do notice them, they are not convincing. To see a miracle as something significant, we must first believe in its significance. If we do not believe that an event can have meaning, then we will not see anything miraculous. The power of a miracle as a proof is not inherent in the miracle itself; it is contingent upon our readiness to accept the phenomenon as a miracle. If we do not want to see it as a miracle, we will not; it will be a coincidence, an unexplained phenomenon, or just something that happened—but there it will stop. If I do believe that events are significant, that they have some meaning beyond the mere fact of their existence, then I do not need extraordinary, supernatural phenomena in order to see miracles. If I am ready for miracles, I can walk down the street and see sunshine, and that is enough of a miracle. If I am not ready for miracles, seeing thirty dancing angels will not do anything to me. I will take a picture, send it to the newspaper, and that will be the end of that.

Incidentally, that is true about almost everything, in every realm of knowledge. First, we have to believe that a fact or a chain of events is significant; only then can we interpret the events. If we do not search for meaning, then things just happen; why shouldn't they? My late uncle was sitting in a train, reading a popular book on science. After some time, the person sitting across from him said, "You look like an intelligent person; why do you read such foolish books? Look at the title!" The title was *Why Does Fire Burn?* My uncle asked, "What's wrong with it?" The stranger replied, "What kind of a question is that? If you do not light a fire, it will not burn; if you light it, why shouldn't it burn?" If a particular question does not make any sense, then we will not care. One cannot go any further than that point, in any field, whether in science, politics, theology, or anything else. The attempt to connect ideas or events into a significant order is contingent upon the notion that such an order exists.

To illustrate this point, let us consider the very idea of the written word. Someone who can read will try to decipher a line of writing in another language, even when it is full of strange characters. For someone who is not familiar with the notion of writing, and has never seen writing before, the words will be smudges on a page, and nothing more. Unless you are ready, beforehand, to accept that a particular question has significance, you will not ask it.

In that sense, the miracles, whether they appear supernatural, natural, or simply ordinary, are full of meaning if
I am ready to "read the book." Unless I believe that there
is a message, I will never try to find out what is in the
message. If someone were to ask, "What is the message of
this chair?" I would say that there is no meaning in it. I
would not even try to find out why it has this form. If I
did believe that it carries some message, then it would be
a very different question. It is not a fact that would
change my mind; it is my mind that would interpret the
facts. My notions about what to search for will determine
which questions I will ask.

Other people, of a more intellectual bent, search for
God through philosophical proofs. There are numerous
proofs in many books of pure philosophy or theology.
However, no proof for the existence or nonexistence of
God is convincing,[4] if one does not want to be convinced.
It is impossible to turn a person who does not want to believe into a believer. Nothing that person sees anywhere,
in any way, will convince him to believe unless he is prepared to accept it as proof. If he is not prepared, rightly or
wrongly, no proof will have any power or meaning. Even if
you bring proof to such a person, the response will be, "So
what? What significance does *that* have?"

That readiness to accept new arguments and proofs depends on a person's former convictions is a notion not
confined to the realm of belief; it exists also in other walks
of life. A lawyer describes in his memoirs how he experienced such a situation.[5] He was an apprentice in the dis-

trict attorney's office, and was given the job of prosecuting a certain case. In the middle of the process, he finished his training, and entered into private practice as a junior lawyer. The first case he was given was to defend the same person he had just been prosecuting. "Then," he said, "I began to understand the subjectivity involved. The evidence was the same, but suddenly I was compelled to take the other side, and that changed my mental process."

This is not just a problem for lawyers; everywhere, one can find out that no one is as deaf as the person who does not want to listen. With all that, it should be remembered that proof, or belief, has very little to do with reality. If I describe a giraffe to a person with a skeptical turn of mind, he might say that it is an unreasonable concept; giraffes do not seem like reasonable creatures at all. It is unlikely, so he does not believe in it. Does the giraffe care whether we believe in it or not? Whether we believe or not certainly does not affect the giraffe. The planet Mars, the Andromeda galaxy, and the giraffe will all exist whether we believe in them or not. They probably do not even care much whether we do or do not believe in them. In the same way, God's existence is not dependent on our belief or disbelief, nor on proofs, one way or the other.

Of course, it is very difficult to accept a notion that is not grounded in our own experience. Because of the tendency to project known facts onto the unknown, we become entangled in our limited knowledge. There is a parable in Arabic literature that applies here (although originally used for a very different purpose). An old philosopher was stranded on an island with a young disciple. He raised the boy and taught him everything he knew. When the boy grew up, he asked the philosopher, "How did we come into the world?" The old man described the process to him. The young man, in spite of his well-trained politeness, said, "What you tell me is such a tall tale that it cannot be believed. I know from my own experience and experimentation that if I did not breathe for two minutes, I would die. Now you are telling me that I existed for nine months without breathing! That is clearly a logical impossibility, and it is clear proof that the whole tale is an invention."

The point is that even if a theory is unlikely, that says nothing at all about reality. Whether or not we believe it and can explain it, whether we think it is reasonable or entirely irrational, babies are born. If something exists, it exists, whether we believe in it or not, whether we can prove its existence or not. If it is, it is. No matter how reasonable or unlikely I think they are, my opinion does not have any impact on the real facts. We can try to explain them one way or another, but our explanations have nothing to do with reality.

However, even though our belief—or lack of it—may not matter to God, it matters a great deal to us. Belief changes our attitudes, our ways of coping with reality, and how we behave, and that is why there is such urgency to the question.

Religion is a formal relationship between humans and

God. Some people may adhere to it out of deep conviction; others may accept it as a convenience, as an accepted norm in society, or just through inertia. Belief is more informal, and probably far more common. On the other hand, for most people—barring a few exceptional individuals—belief is also less constant. When our lives are more or less normal, we do not have the time or inclination to think about God. When we are happy and content, we may occasionally say, "Thank God," but it is usually a mere phrase that means very little. In times of disaster or other disruption, a very powerful and compelling need for meaning appears; it is not always belief, but it is at least a desire for belief. Sometimes people find themselves in a position in which they have to have a God, whether He exists or not. Someone who was caught in an earthquake once described it, "The greatest need I had then was to have something to believe in—a God or an idol—but something that I could adhere to, because the world was collapsing."

When the world collapses physically, financially, or personally, we have a great need for something that will not be destroyed along with the general destruction. That "something," although not always a comfort, and not always an answer, nevertheless meets the need for permanence and reliability. Therefore, in times of personal or general disaster, there is a surge in belief. From a philosophical point of view, however, disaster is not an argument for belief. Even on a theological level, it is not a very good reason, however understandable on the human level.

The crisis-inspired belief is a particular experience; usually, when the crisis passes, the belief passes also. Sometimes, people are embarrassed by their sudden belief, but even if not, it is usually a transient mode, not a permanent change.

Hard times and good times do not prove anything about God, but they show that the quest surges and diminishes according to our situation. What happens to people in hard times shows that there is an inner source of belief that is revealed when one needs or wants it. In such times, people who had forgotten their childhood prayers for many years suddenly remember them. Even those who have never prayed, and surely did not intend to, try to formulate some way of appealing to the Almighty. The remarkable side of this phenomenon is not in the need, but in the fact that inside the "nonbeliever" there is enough belief to hang his hopes on. In the same way, when a person in distress cries out, "Mommy!" it does not prove that he has a mother, or that his mother will help him. It does prove that there is, in that person, a deep attachment—and trust.

This inner belief can be dismissed through any number of rational explanations. It can be called primitive, reflecting ancient fears and hopes, yet rationalization does not make the emotion disappear. Like many other primordial emotions, it has the same quality of being a natural, integral part of what we are. Hunger, fear, sexual attraction, and desire for companionship all share this same quality. Even if one is able to ignore them temporarily, they cannot be eradicated. More than that, such basic desires and emotions, which exist prior to and regardless of any specific cultural influences, are a part of the very definition of humanity itself. These are connected to a very essential part of our mind, and are the basis for any cognitive process in us. These basic parts of ourselves can be somewhat modulated and regulated, bound by rationalistic links and limitations, but they cannot be ignored.

Belief in God can be naïve and childish, or sophisticated and elaborate. The images we have of God may be nonsensical, or well constructed philosophically. Yet the essence of this belief, when stripped of verbiage and frills, is simply: existence makes some sense. Sometimes, one may think—probably mistakenly—that one knows exactly what that sense is, while others may just ponder it. In any case, there is a firm belief—which precedes any kind of thought, rational and irrational—that there is some sense in things. What we experience, through our senses or inwardly, are only disjointed pieces. The fact that we somehow connect these particles of information stems from our a priori faith that there is a connection—because it precedes reason.

Accepting this assumption is the first, most fundamental "leap of faith"; not an experience, but a belief. Of course, people would not call this "religious belief," nor see it as a point of faith. Nevertheless, when analyzed properly, it becomes—for those people who are afraid of the word—frightfully close to believing in God. This belief is like our belief in the existence of the world: it is the foundation of our relation to everything; indeed, on some levels, it is perhaps even more fundamental.[6] This deep, native belief can be found when we "undo" our childhood training and eliminate everything we were taught about belief as children. Then we must answer the question "What is God?" not on a philosophical level that claims objective definitions, but as an attempt at least to understand "What is God for me?" To do this, we have to get rid of our preconceived and learned structures and images, which blur our real belief. We must delve very deeply into ourselves, into our most primal thinking, indeed—to begin at the beginning.

The very first beginning of our thinking occurs long before we are born. Fetuses do think, as they have a rather developed brain in the last months of pregnancy. There is even scientific evidence that babies dream in utero—they have electrical brain patterns compatible with dreaming. What does a fetus dream about? That may, perhaps, never be answered completely; we surely forget our prenatal dreams, whatever they are. What does a fetus think about? It may have the first stirrings of consciousness of self, because as much as it is still a part of its mother's body, it has a brain and a mind of its own. However, the only thing a fetus could possibly think about is theology. Using this term in this context seems, at best, facetious. Obviously, a fetus does not formulate its thought in words, because the mind of a fetus is a pre-mind, not a conscious mind that uses words. Words become significant only in adulthood (and sometimes not even then). However, theology does not always mean heavy terminology written in ponderous manner (and never read). Basically, it is knowledge of God—or any system of thinking about the Divine.

To a fetus, who has almost no outside experience, there may be just two points of thought. One may, perhaps, be "me," and the other, "all." The only thing that exists is the wholeness. If we put it into words, it would be something like "I am engulfed within the wholeness of existence; in me and beyond me is this wholeness. This is the food and the shelter, the matrix of everything, infinity." At a much later stage, we may say that it was the mother's womb, but for the fetus, it is the universe, the everything in which it exists. We begin life with the experience of undifferentiated wholeness. When the baby is born, it is faced with a myriad of disconnected details, each of which demands to be observed, and somehow integrated into the mind.* In a way, the baby seems to forget what it had known before.† Later, as we mature, our ability to piece together meaning in life is based on that prenatal experience.

*That is the stage in which every baby shifts from pure theology into epistemology—namely, defining perception, noting the difference between true and false, finding out the basic meaning of existing things.

†The same idea is described in the Talmud (Tractate Niddah 30b), in a far more poetical way. There it is written that the fetus is having the happiest time of life, in which it sees the whole world and studies Torah. When the baby is born, an angel slaps it, and makes it forget everything.

The belief that things somehow fit together into a whole that makes sense is the most primitive, most basic belief, and paradoxically, it is also possibly the most sophisticated and abstract belief. It is so very basic that it precedes doctrine. Although it is not a definition of God, the notion that somehow the world makes sense, that there is a background upon which everything exists, is so simple and so taken for granted, that we do not even realize that it is the root of all belief. This very basic thought-emotion is sometimes felt by adults in special circumstances. Freud used the expression "the oceanic emotion" to describe this feeling that people sometimes experience when facing the ocean: the vastness, the power, the attraction.

As far as we know, this is also the faith of most primitive tribes: a monistic or monotheistic notion of the Whole. Polytheism is neither fundamental nor basic, but rather a more advanced attempt to differentiate, to cut this basic notion of a unified wholeness into discrete parts that are more concrete, and that can easily be defined and identified. This development is also destructive, as it breaks our basic intuitive understanding into pieces. To make sense, polytheism has to develop mythologies and explanations for each separate entity. It takes many generations to return to a unified view.[7]

Ultimately, high theology and high philosophy can only answer the question "What is God?" with the answer of a newborn baby, "God is the wholeness of everything." The mystical writings say things about God that every child knows. In the words of the *Zohar,* "God, You are the completeness of everything."[8] The understanding of God as "the completeness of everything" is quite simple, and it is not an anthropomorphic picture of God. It is not an image that people can visualize. This understanding is so close and integral that it is almost invisible.

On the other hand, it is a very abstract notion, and difficult to express in words. Children are usually too young to articulate their belief, and by the time they develop consciousness and language, they can see the world only as disjointed pieces. Perhaps earlier, the child understands the oneness, and if no one spoils that belief, he will have it, wherever and however he lives. The secret of belief is not to expect to see miracles, or to have grand mystical experiences, but rather, to preserve the innate notion we are born with.

Instead of adding, we have to edit out so many extra, useless words and ideas. If we can come to the core, and carefully develop the very fundamental points of our minds, we may discover that God has always existed within us.

Notes

❦

Words

1. The paraphrase is taken from *Midrash Genesis Rabbah* 8:4.
2. *Genesis Rabbah* 17:4.
3. *Genesis Rabbah* 17:4.
4. *Midrash Tanḥuma, Shemini,* 8.
5. Rabbi Yehonathan Eibeschutz (1690–1764), *Ya'arot Devash* (Hebrew), Part 2, Homily 12.
6. See, for instance, the book *You Just Don't Understand* by Deborah Tannen.
7. *Midrash Leviticus Rabbah* 17:1, which, incidentally, is not very different from what is written in Plato's *Symposium.*

Nature

1. See *Avot de-Rabbi Nathan* (an expansion of *Pirkei Avot,* "The Ethics of Our Fathers," a tractate of the Mishnah that deals with moral and ethical guidance), Chapter 16.
2. See *Midrash Tanḥuma, Tazri'a* 5.
3. Babylonian Talmud, Tractate *Eruvin* 100b, based on Job 35:11.
4. See *Sefer ha-'Ikkarim* by Rabbi Joseph Elbo (a book presenting arguments to prove the eternal nature of the Torah), Part 3, Chapter 1.
5. *Avot de-Rabbi Nathan,* Chapter 1.

Good

1. As the hero of the novelette "Tobermory" by Saki (H. H. Munro).

2. See Proverbs 12:15.

3. Proverbs 16:2, and elsewhere.

4. In a Russian novel (*The Thief* by Leonid Leonov, written in 1931), there is a psychological discussion about the fate of a successful soldier of the revolution who cannot readjust to normal civilian society.

5. Babylonian Talmud, Tractate *Makkot* 24a; this section contains some other pertinent examples.

6. Ca. 70 B.C.E.–ca. 10 C.E., one of the leading Jewish scholars of all times.

7. Babylonian Talmud, Tractate *Shabbat* 31a.

8. Rashi, on the Talmud, Tractate *Shabbat* 31a.

9. In *Critique of Pure Reason*.

10. Genesis 9:1–7. In the Bible, these laws are not entirely clear; see Babylonian Talmud, Tractate *Sanhedrin* 56b–60a, which contains a more elaborate description of them.

11. *Pirkei Avot* ("The Ethics of Our Fathers") 5:10.

Faith

1. In the times of Amenhotep IV (called also Akhenaton) and his successor, Tutankhamen.

2. Both modern philosophy and modern mathematics began with the work of Descartes. His analytic method of thinking focused attention on the problem of how we know, which has occupied philosophers ever since. His *Discourse on Method* was published in 1637.

3. In *The Varieties of Religious Experience*.

Good Deeds

1. From the repetition of the *Musaf* prayer for the High Holy Days.

2. Babylonian Talmud, Tractate *Yoma* 69b.

Sex

1. See some discussions about this in "Conversations with Lenin" by Clara Zetkin (1852–1933), in *Erinnerung an Lenin*, Verlag für Literatur und Politik, Wien, 1929.

2. Yet see, for example, the writings of Konrad Lorenz, the animal ethologist; e.g., *King Solomon's Ring*, Crowell, NY, 1952.

3. E.g., Rabbi Ovadiah Seforno (Italy, 1470–1540).

4. See Proverbs 9:17, and far more elaboration in the Babylonian Talmud, Tractate *Sanhedrin* 75a.

Death

1. Babylonian Talmud, Tractate *Berakhot* 8a; Tractate *Mo'ed Katan* 28a; Tractate *Ketubot* 77b.

2. The most comprehensive collection of Jewish sources on this subject can be found in the book *Gesher ha-Ḥayyim*, by Rabbi Y.M. Tokachinsky, private publisher, Jerusalem, 1960 (see especially volume II, Chapter 27). If there is any truth whatsoever in spiritualistic sessions, then they must be contacts with souls at such an intermediate stage.

3. See, for instance, the book *Shivḥei ha-Besht* ("Praises of the Ba'al Shem Tov," the history and praises of Rabbi Israel Ba'al Shem Tov, the founder of the Hassidic movement; Hebrew, originally published in Kapost, 1815). This book contains stories about souls thus caught in *'Olam ha-Dimyon*.

4. The origin of the expression is Biblical: I Samuel 25:29; see also Babylonian Talmud, Tractate *Shabbat* 152b; *Zohar* (the major Jewish Kabbalistic book), Part I, 217b; and elsewhere.

5. This point is somewhat discussed in *Sefer ha-'Ikkarim* by Rabbi Yosef Elbo, Section 4, Chapter 33.

6. See *Torat ha-Adam, Sha'ar ha-Gemul* ("The Doctrine of Man," chapter on reward and punishment; Hebrew) by Nahmanides (1194–1270), where he discusses many aspects of life after death.

7. Barring a few exceptions; see Babylonian Talmud, Tractates *Rosh Hashanah* 17a, *Bava Metzi'a* 58b, and many other places.

8. Babylonian Talmud, Tractate *Shabbat* 33b.

9. Maimonides, Preface to his Commentary on *Pirkei Avot* ("The Ethics of Our Fathers").

10. Babylonian Talmud, Tractate *Berakhot* 64a.

Envy

1. *HaYom Yom,* the collected sayings of Rabbi Yosef Yitzhak Schneerson, the sixth Lubavitcher Rebbe.

2. In his Preface to the Commentary on *Pirkei Avot* ("The Ethics of Our Fathers").

3. See *Tikkunei Zohar* (a section of the Zohar), page 19b.

4. *Midrash Genesis Rabbah* 12:8; *Leviticus Rabbah* 9:9.

5. Babylonian Talmud, Tractate *Bava Batra* 22b.

6. Rabbi Yaakov Yitzchak Rabinowitz (1765–1814).

Masks

1. There is a wonderful book by Johan Huizinga on the notion of play, called *Homo Ludens* (Beacon Press, Boston, 1955). Though it may not be easy reading, it discusses a very important cultural notion.

2. See the theatrical representation of it in Richard Brinsley Sheridan's eighteenth-century comedy *The School for Scandal,* as well as in many contemporary literary and art reviews.

3. See, for example, "The Happy Hypocrite," in *The Happy Hypocrite* by Max Beerbohm (1872–1956), Green Tiger Press, La Jolla, Calif., 1985.

4. *Midrash Ecclesiastes Rabbah* 12:9; *Midrash* on Psalms, Psalm 9.

5. Mishnah, Tractate *Peah,* 8:9.

6. *Midrash Exodus Rabbah,* 5:9.

Friends

1. In his preface to *Pirkei Avot* ("The Ethics of Our Fathers").

Family

1. A very good fictional description of such a state can be found in Aldous Huxley's *Brave New World.*

2. In his *General Introduction to Psychoanalysis.*

Love

1. The *Tanya* (the fundamental book of Chabad, written by the founder of Chabad, Rabbi Schneur Zalman of Lyady), Chapter 9, and many other writings by the same author.

2. *Pirkei Avot* ("The Ethics of Our Fathers") 5:16.

3. See 2 Samuel 13:1–19.

God

1. These last two lines are, in fact, a quotation from the *Zohar* (the fundamental Jewish Kabbalistic text), *Tikkunei Zohar* page 17a.

2. See the commentary of Rabbi Avraham Ibn Ezra on Exodus, Chapter 20.

3. *Mishneh Torah* (Maimonides' major work, which contains all of Jewish law), *Hilkhot Yesodei ha-Torah,* 8:1.

4. The subject has been well defined in Kant's *Critique of Pure Reason,* in which he deals with these proofs in his list of antinomies.

5. Sammy Groeneman (1875–1952), *Memoirs of a Yekke (German Jew)* (Hebrew, Am Oved, Tel Aviv 1946).

6. See Descartes' *Discourse on Method.*

7. Compare this with the view expressed by Maimonides in *Mishneh Torah, Sefer ha-Mada', Hilkhot 'Avodah Zarah,* Chapter 1.

8. *Tikkunei Zohar,* page 17b.

This book has been prepared with the assistance of
the Israel Institute for Talmudic Publications.